INSIDER'S GUIDE TO

DOLL BUYING & SELLING

by Jan Foulke
Photographs by Howard Foulke

D0188140

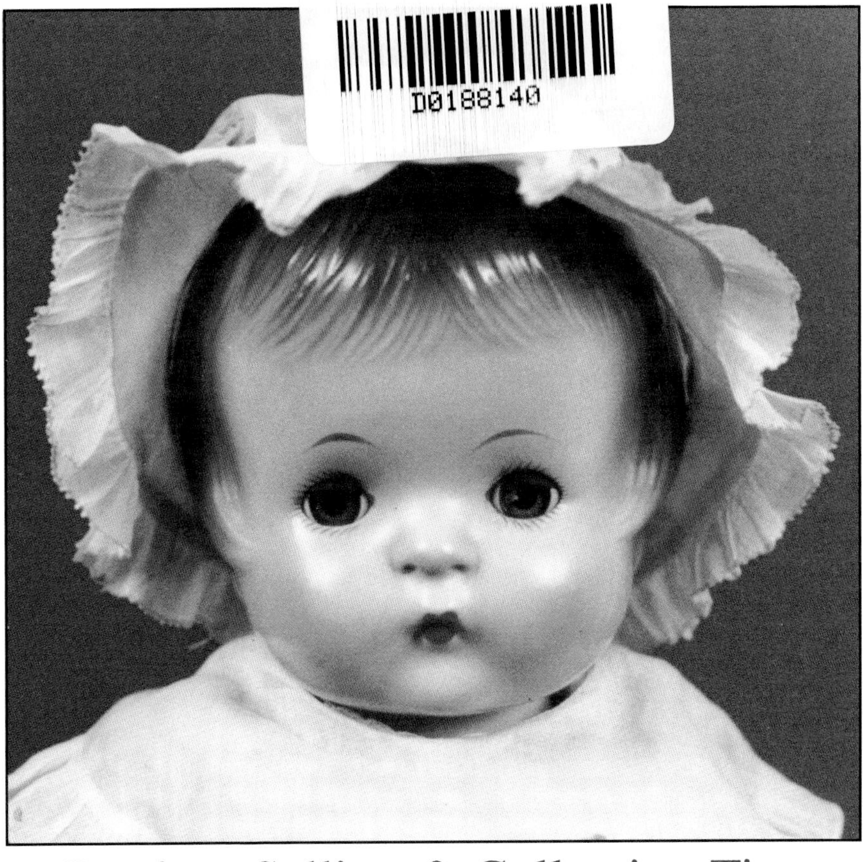

Buying, Selling & Collecting Tips

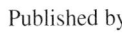

Published by Hobby House Press

Hobby House Press, Inc.
Grantsville, Maryland 21536

Other Titles by Author:

Blue Book of Dolls & Values®
2nd Blue Book of Dolls & Values®
3rd Blue Book of Dolls & Values®
4th Blue Book of Dolls & Values®
5th Blue Book of Dolls & Values®
6th Blue Book of Dolls & Values®
7th Blue Book of Dolls & Values®
8th Blue Book of Dolls & Values®
9th Blue Book of Dolls & Values®
10th Blue Book of Dolls & Values®
11th Blue Book of Dolls & Values®
12th Blue Book of Dolls & Values®

Focusing on Effanbee Composition Dolls
Focusing on Treasury of Mme. Alexander Dolls
Focusing on Gebrüder Heubach Dolls
Kestner: King of Dollmakers
Simon & Halbig Dolls: The Artful Aspect
Doll Classics
Focusing on Dolls
China Doll Collecting
German 'Dolly' Collecting

COVER: 17in (43cm) Shirley Temple, 1957. *H & J Foulke, Inc.* 15in (38cm) Kley & Hahn 525 Toddler. *H & J Foulke, Inc.*

TITLE PAGE: 19in (48cm) Effanbee composition *Patsy Ann* from the popular Patsy family of dolls ranging from 6in (15cm) *Wee Patsy* to 30in (76cm) *Patsy Mae*. *Patsy Ann* is all original and in excellent condition with rosy cheeks, clear eyes and perfect eyelashes. 1928+. *H & J Foulke, Inc.*

BACK COVER: If you saw this 18in (46cm) doll marked A 9 T in an antique show, would you pay $650 for it? If you did, you could have made a $40,000 profit. Although she seems dilapidated, she just needs some "TLC." Her head is perfect with no cracks, chips or abrasions. Her body is very good with only normal wear at joints and on toes. The elastic needs to be replaced, which will tighten her joints; this is a fairly simple process. Clean her original wig and shift, find her appropriate old clothing, shoes and socks, and she will be a beauty, the star of any collection. For proof, see her sister on page 20. *H & J Foulke, Inc.*

© 1995 by Jan and Howard Foulke

Printed in the United States of America

ISBN: 0-87588-442-3

TABLE OF CONTENTS

Questions from Collectors – Answers from an Insider

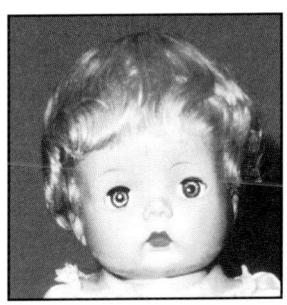

A rare find!

*A printed cloth
cut & sew doll!*

*The importance of
hang tags...*

TABLE OF CONTENTS
Questions from Collectors – Answers from an Insider

Unlock the magic of an Alexander doll!

The Kewpie cuties... in production since 1912.

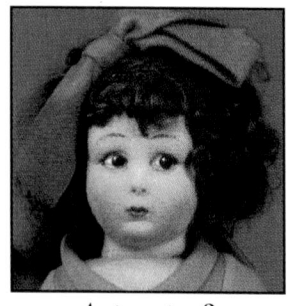

Art or toy?

INTRODUCTION

23in (58cm) German girl with bisque head and composition body, mold number 1912, produced by the German firm of Cuno & Otto Dressel with bisque head poured for them by an unknown porcelain factory. She has "real" upper eyelashes as well as painted ones. She is typical of millions of dolls of this type, known to collectors as "dolly faces," which were imported into the United States. Ca. 1900. *H & J Foulke, Inc.*

After many years of listening to questions about doll collecting and receiving letters requesting general doll collecting advice, we are finally getting around to writing this little book all about doll collecting. It comes from our nearly 25 years inside doll collecting and our 20 years of making a living in the doll world.

Many people who know us only through the *Blue Book of Dolls & Values®*, which we have been writing for over 20 years, do not realize that we are doll dealers with a large world-wide business. We are busily involved in the doll world on a daily basis. We exhibit our dolls at major doll shows, the National Antique Doll Dealers Association shows, and the United Federation of Doll Clubs (UFDC) National. We sell a large number of dolls by mail through our monthly doll list. We attend major auctions, conventions and other doll activities to keep our fingers on the pulse of the doll world. A lot of what we have learned and observed about doll collecting is revealed in this little book. We hope it helps you to be comfortable and happy inside doll collecting also.

Jan Foulke

Antique Dolls:

Generally dolls more than 75 years old, although bisque dolls produced through the 1930s are considered antiques. Principal materials of dolls included are wood, papier-mâché/composition, wax, china, parian, bisque, cloth and metal.

18in (46cm) German Patent Washable (composition) lady doll in original clothing, pristine condition.Ca. 1880+. *Kay & Wayne Jensen Collection.*

Collectible Dolls:

Generally dolls between 30 and 75 years old, although American composition dolls from the 1910 decade are considered collectible. Principal materials of dolls included are composition, wood, cloth, hard plastic and vinyl.

23in (58cm) unmarked American "mama doll" with composition shoulder head, arms and lower legs, cloth torso and upper legs, original clothing, in very good condition. Ca. 1925+. This type of doll has a voice box in the torso which cries "mama" when the doll is tipped, hence the term "mama doll." *H & J Foulke, Inc.*

Modern Dolls:

Generally dolls less than 30 years old, including dolls made for collectors as well as play dolls. These are also called **contemporary dolls**. Principal materials of dolls included are cloth, wood, hard plastic, vinyl and bisque.

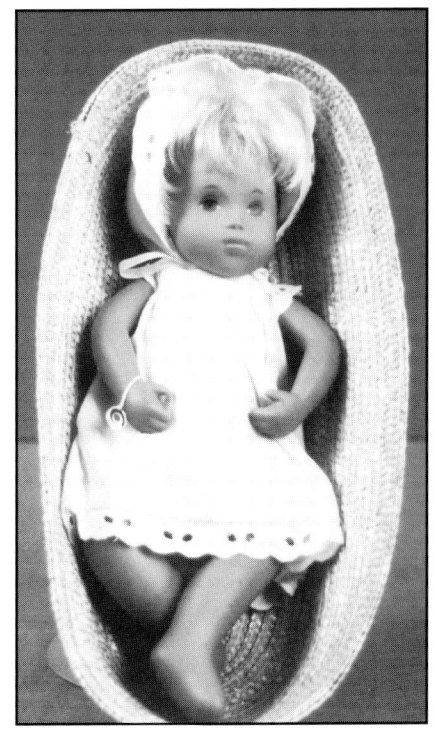

12in (31cm) vinyl *Sasha Baby* made in England, original clothing and basket with wrist tag, excellent condition. Sexed *Sasha Babies* were made before 1979; unsexed babies date from 1979-1986.

Artist Dolls:

Original dolls of the past 50 years which were created as works of art and decorative objects, not intended as playthings. Principal materials used are bisque, china, wood, cloth, vinyl, Fimo®, Cernit, resin and Sculpey®.

16in (41cm) *Holly*, a Victorian child, designed by artist Fawn Zeller and made by the United States Historical Society of Richmond, Virginia. in 1983, has bisque head, lower arms and lower legs, and cloth torso. *H & J Foulke, Inc.*

HOW DO I GET STARTED?

The answer to this question is not as simple as it seems. There is a lot more to doll collecting than simply going out and buying a doll! The doll field is actually very broad, spanning more than a 300-year time period – from the quaint English wooden dolls of the 1690s William and Mary period to the modern artist dolls of the 1990s. When you realize that you are inexorably drawn to dolls, explore the whole spectrum a little to see which dolls "speak" to you the loudest. Whereas 20-25 years ago there were actually few places to see dolls, the doll world has exploded to such an extent within the last ten years that dolls are now much more readily available.

Museums

If you think antique dolls may be your field, visit museums that have educational displays of old dolls. Some museums are simply for entertainment, displaying dolls in cute little scenes that tell nothing about the dolls. To do some serious viewing, schedule vacation trips to places such as the Margaret Woodbury Strong Museum in Rochester, New York; the Rosalie Whyle Museum of Doll Art in Bellevue, Washington; the Mary Merritt Doll Museum in Douglassville, Pennsylvania; the Wenham Museum in Wenham, Massachusetts; the Yesteryear's Doll Museum in Sandwich, Massachusetts; and the Shelburne Museum in Vermont.

These are just a few museums that I have enjoyed visiting, but there are others throughout the country. Call any museums in your area or in any cities you are visiting to see if they have doll collections and if the collections are on display. Many do have dolls, but be skeptical of their information because most general museum curators know little about dolls. Sadly, most curators do not bother to get a doll expert to review their collections and assist in preparation of exhibit information.

Look...and fall in love!

OPPOSITE PAGE: A spectacular Kämmer & Reinhardt German bisque-head character child, mold #102. The K & R series of character children are among the highest priced German dolls. K & R pioneered the character doll movement, which started in 1909. *Private Collection.*

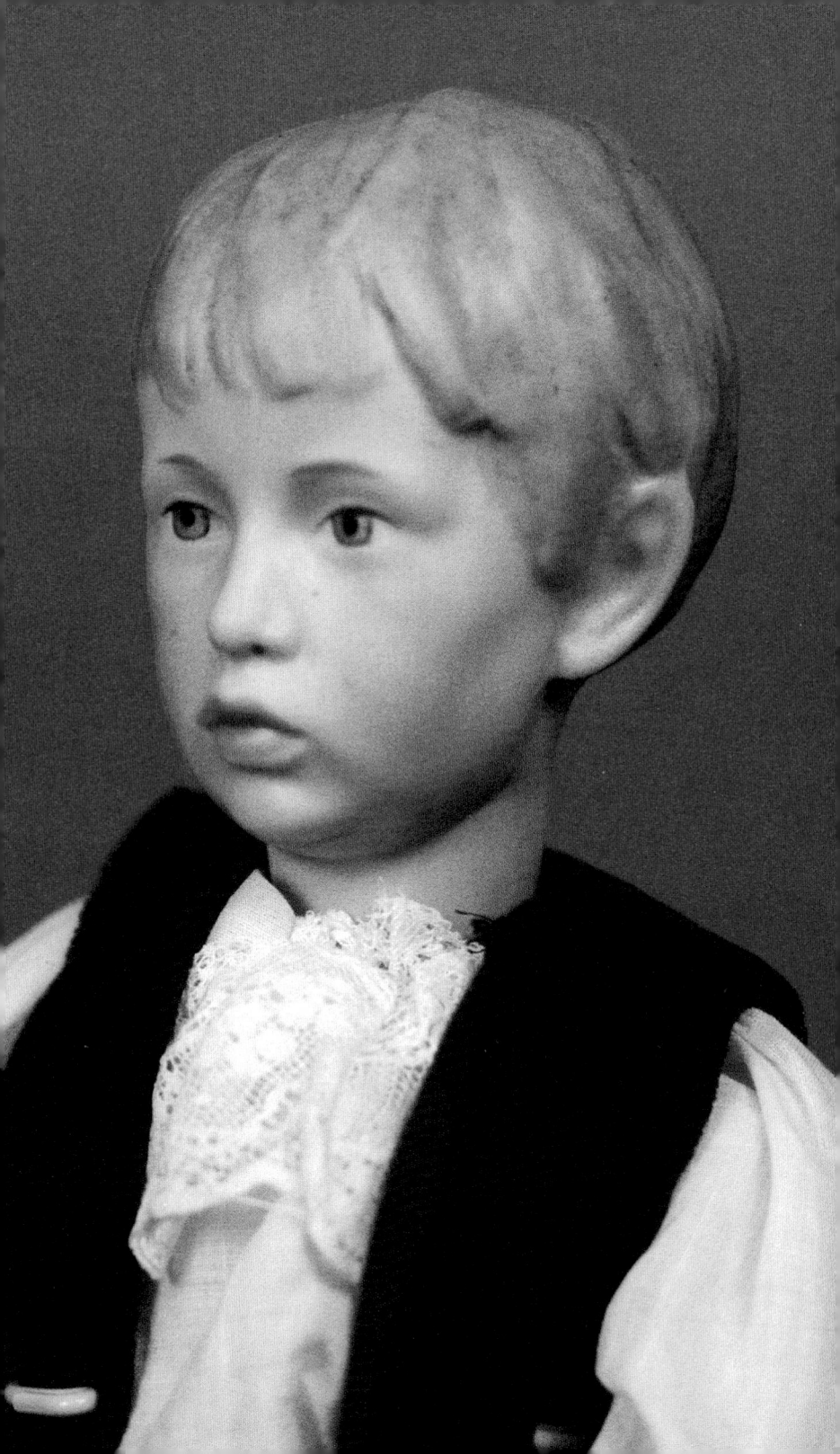

Shows and Stores

17in (43cm) all-cloth *Bambino* by Mabel Lucie Attwell for the Chad Valley Co. of Birmingham, England. The original cotton print dress contains Attwell designs, and the glass eyes look to the side. A very hard-to-find doll. Ca. 1930. *H & J Foulke, Inc.*

Of course, the best place to see a variety of dolls is at one of the large doll shows. Some of the smaller doll shows are good for collectible and modern dolls, but the larger shows have a greater number of dealers in antique dolls. The Gaithersburg, Maryland show is held four times a year and is one of the oldest and best doll shows. The facility is dirty and run down, but there is lots of good stuff to see and buy. In the Chicago area, several promoters offer doll and toy shows at the Kane County Fairgrounds. In the San Francisco area, several large shows a year are held at the Vallejo Fair Grounds. Other shows throughout the country are advertised in *Doll Reader*®, *Dolls, Antique Doll World,* and other doll collector oriented magazines.

The National Association of Antique Doll Dealers (NADDA) Show in Wilmington, Delaware, every fall is a "must go" event for collectors of antique dolls and older collectibles with a cut-off date of 1955. The NADDA Show won the prestigious "Jumeau Award" in 1994 for "Best Doll Show in the World." There are several other NADDA Shows throughout the country, but the Wilmington one is the largest. It is well worth traveling to this show. The Wilmington show is also advantageous because there is **no sales tax** in Delaware.

I think the most prestigious show of all, if you can possibly get to it, is the United Federation of Doll Clubs (UFDC) Annual Convention. This show is open to the public for one afternoon and is well worth the $10 admission fee. The dealers in the UFDC sales room present antique, collectible, modern and artist dolls. The UFDC Convention is held in a different major city each July or August. If you call UFDC Headquarters in Kansas City, Missouri; the receptionist will give you information on the public day's location and date. It is a worthwhile show to attend even if it is a several days' journey for you.

In addition to attending shows, you should check any antique shops, flea markets or antique markets in your area and inquire about anyone who might deal in dolls. Many doll specialists have booths at antique mar-

18in (46cm) *Grape Lady* by Emma Clear. This is a reproduction of a German china doll of the 1850s. Mrs. Clear's dolls are well-respected by collectors. Ca. 1948. *H & J Foulke, Inc.*

kets, and some general dealers have a few dolls. In a later chapter we will describe in more detail the process of buying dolls from dealers and auctions. For now, we are simply suggesting places where you might find and see dolls.

If you are looking for stores that sell artist dolls, *BARBIE*® dolls, Madame Alexanders or other modern dolls, check the yellow pages of your local phone book under "toys" or "dolls." Call the shops listed and ask which types and lines of dolls they carry. When you go into a department store, always ask whether or not the store has a toy or doll department. Many large stores are doing away with their toy departments and putting dolls in the gift department or children's clothing section.

> ## *Flea markets and antique shops*
> ## *are great sources...*

Books and Magazines

As you are deciding what dolls you might want to collect, you should start doing some studying. Doll magazines might be the place to start. *Doll Reader®, Dolls, Antique Doll World* and *Contemporary Doll Collector* are probably the leading ones. A lot of newsstands now carry these magazines. The first two contain material on antique, collectible, and modern dolls and paper dolls. *Antique Doll World* emphasizes antique dolls, and *Contemporary Doll Collector* emphasizes modern artist dolls, although it too is beginning to have a few articles on antique and collectible dolls.

If you decide to collect dolls, the first investment you should make is in some reliable doll books. I don't think you can have too many books on dolls. I have about 32 feet of doll books. I am always buying books on all types of dolls! But I like books that give me information about dolls, not just pretty picture books. I want to learn as much as possible. I don't want to see dolls surrounded by flowers. I want to see good, clear close-ups of the dolls themselves. One caution about buying older books on dolls. Much new doll information has been uncovered in the past ten years, making much of the material in older books inaccurate and outdated. So, do be careful about what you take as "gospel." In any growing field, more and more information becomes available all of the time – much of the new information negating the old information.

12in (31cm) Italian felt children *Little Homemaker* and *Shoe-Shine*, in the Lenci style, not marked. All original with accessories, nice clean condition. Ca. 1930. *H & J Foulke, Inc.*

If you are collecting pre-1930 dolls, *The Collector's Encyclopedia of Dolls, Volumes I & II* by the Colemans (Dorothy S., Elizabeth Ann and Evelyn Jane) is indispensable. If you are on a limited budget, buy Volume II as your starting point because it is the most comprehensive. For modern dolls dating from before 1974, *Twentieth Century Dolls* and *More Twentieth Century Dolls* by Johana Gast Anderton are good basic references. Then of course, you must buy my **Blue Book of Dolls & Values**®. Not only does it give doll values and advice about buying dolls, it also provides lots of information about specific dolls, as well as over 500 doll photographs

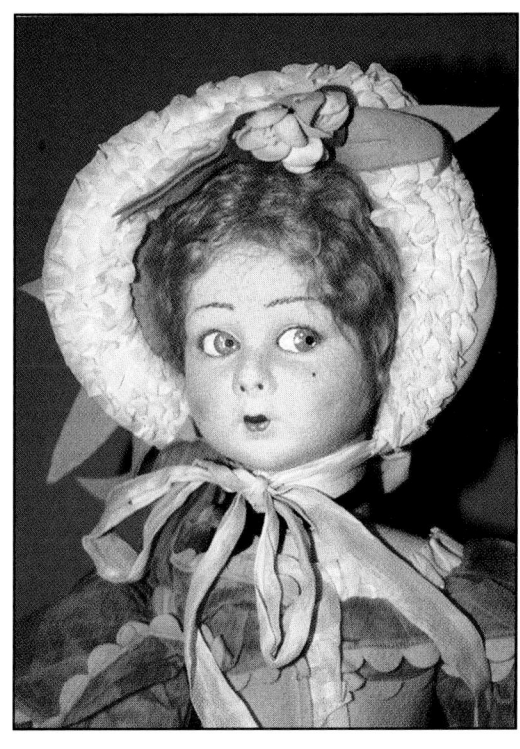

36in (91cm) felt long-limbed boudoir doll by the Italian Lenci firm; clean and all original with good color. Ca. 1920+. *Richard Wright Antiques.*

(none with flowers) – the next best thing to actually seeing the dolls themselves. The **Blue Book** is the first book that most new doll collectors buy. It has prices for antique, collectible, artist dolls and modern dolls.

Most bookstores, including Walden, Borders and Dalton, have a few books on dolls, but they may not have the best ones. The most comprehensive selection of the best books on dolls is available by mail through Hobby House Press. You will also find books on dolls as you visit doll shows and museums. Dealers who sell books can recommend the best books in the area of doll collecting you choose to study.

You can never have too many doll books!

Should I Collect Dolls? Am I Too Old for Dolls?

7in (18cm) German all-bisque googly by J.D. Kestner with unusual jointed elbows and knees, rarely found, appropriately rewigged and redressed. Ca. 1912. *Kay & Wayne Jensen Collection.*

To the seasoned collector this must sound like a frivolous question. But to an adult just beginning to think about collecting, it is a very serious concern. These adults have probably always enjoyed looking at dolls but never had the time or funds to think about collecting. Now they may no longer have families at home and may have more time for themselves.

I know from having a toy store specializing in Madame Alexander Dolls that many adults feel guilty about spending money on dolls for themselves. Many say, "Oh, I wish I had a granddaughter to buy dolls for." Let me assure you that you don't need a granddaughter in order to buy a doll. You can buy one for yourself. It's all right to buy a doll just because you like it and to keep it for yourself. You don't have to give it to a child. I know quite a few adults who buy dolls and say they are for their granddaughters because they can't justify in their own minds buying dolls for themselves. To them I say: admit that you are a doll collector. You'll enjoy buying dolls a lot more, and you'll feel less guilty about it. If you like dolls you *should* collect them. You are never "too old."

You are never too old to collect dolls!

What Should I Collect?

No one can really answer this question for you. You have to decide this on your own. First and foremost, I would advise you to collect dolls that you personally like. Actually, there is nothing that you should or shouldn't collect. Your collection is your hobby and should be based upon your enjoyment of it. Don't let someone else tell you what you should buy or what a doll collection should include. If you like *BARBIE*® dolls, collect them. If your "thing" is Brus, collect them. If you like Alexander dolls, collect them. If you like china head dolls, collect them. I am not a "doll snob." I detest collectors who look down on someone else's collection just because it does not include expensive dolls or antique dolls.

Even though you may have studied dolls before you started your collection, it is very possible that your tastes will change as you become exposed to a greater variety of dolls, and as those of different types begin to grow on you. You may find that you decide to sell or trade some of the dolls that you bought when you first started collecting. This is normal. Nearly everyone comes to that point.

The first antique doll I ever looked at was a *Queen Louise*. I wasn't even into dolls at that time, but I did deal in general antiques. My daughter wanted an antique doll, so I told her I would get her one for Christmas, and I did. It was a Schoenau & Hoffmeister 1909 dolly face. After I purchased her, I bought Colemans' *Collector's Encyclopedia of Dolls* (from Gary Ruddell of Hobby House Press whom I

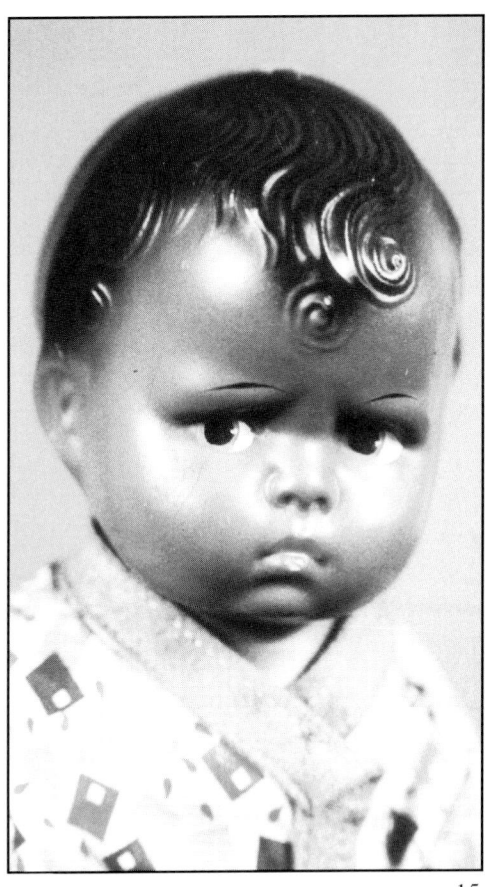

16in (41cm) Effanbee black composition *Grumpy*; composition shoulder head, lower arms and legs, cloth torso and upper limbs, all original outfit, excellent unplayed with condition. *H & J Foulke, Inc.*

15-1/2in (39cm) bisque head googly with chubby jointed composition body from the German porcelain and doll factory of J.D. Kestner, original mohair wig. Ca. 1912. *Private Collection.*

already knew because at that time he sold books on general antiques as well as on dolls) to learn about her. Soon after this experience we got into dolls in a big way. My daughter fell in love with Lenci dolls and started what became a renowned collection of Lenci dolls. To my knowledge, she was the first person to collect them in a big way. She also collected *Ginny* dolls. Both types of dolls were a far cry from the doll we started out with! So, do expect your tastes and interests to undergo some changes.

Some collectors generalize – a little of this and a little of that. They may have a few antique dolls, chinas, papier-mâchés, 1930s and 1940s compositions, even several Sashas and several new Alexander dolls. Some generalize but specialize in one type of doll, such as character babies. Others collect only a particular type of doll, maybe French Fashions or all-bisques, wooden dolls, *Ginnys* or *Shirley Temples.* Some collections are thematic: dolls from literature, celebrity dolls, historical characters, dolls depicting royalty, ballerinas, brides or nuns. The possibilities are practically endless. Thematic collections can span various types and ages of dolls. As I've said before, your collection should be what you like.

It is nice, however, if at least a part of your collection focuses on a particular area. This provides you with an opportunity for specialized study related to the type of dolls you are collecting. Much of our doll knowledge has come from collectors who are willing to share what they have learned with others. For example, a recent article by a collector/dealer in a doll magazine featured an examination of her collection of early so-called almond-eyed Portrait Jumeaux. Her detailed examination shed a lot of new light on what had heretofore been a shadowy area of unmarked Jumeaux. The same has happened in many other areas of doll collecting. A book on Schoenhut dolls by a collector who studied her dolls and those of other collectors brought the full doll production of that company into historical focus. In the area of collectible dolls, such as *Nancy Ann Storybook Dolls* and *Ginny* dolls, collectors have analyzed, compared and come to conclusions about which models are older, what tags different models should have and so on. My own field of specialized collecting is German all-bisque dolls. I have not yet written a book about them, but I plan to. I particularly love the early pouty-faced Kestners. Actually, right now I am looking for one with a swivel-waist. Please let me know if you have one for sale!

Some collectors are more comfortable when they establish parameters for their collections because it forces them to limit their collections. It is just in the nature of some people to want one of everything they see. These people have a hard time with moderation. They have to think long and hard about which aspects of dolls and collecting they enjoy the most. Then they concentrate on these areas to the exclusion of others. For me, the problem areas are paper dolls and doll houses. I love paper dolls. I fondly remember playing for hours and hours with them when I was little. But I feel as though I just cannot let myself get involved in another collecting activity. Another area that could really capture my interest is doll houses and miniatures. But I have limited myself to furniture that will complement my all-bisques. And I do, at the present time, have one German blue roof doll house! Only one, however. I am not getting any more!

12in (31 cm) *Ricky* and *Becky* by artist Astry Campbell, bisque and cloth, original clothing. 1967 & 1968. *H & J Foulke, Inc.*

Are Dolls Good Investments?

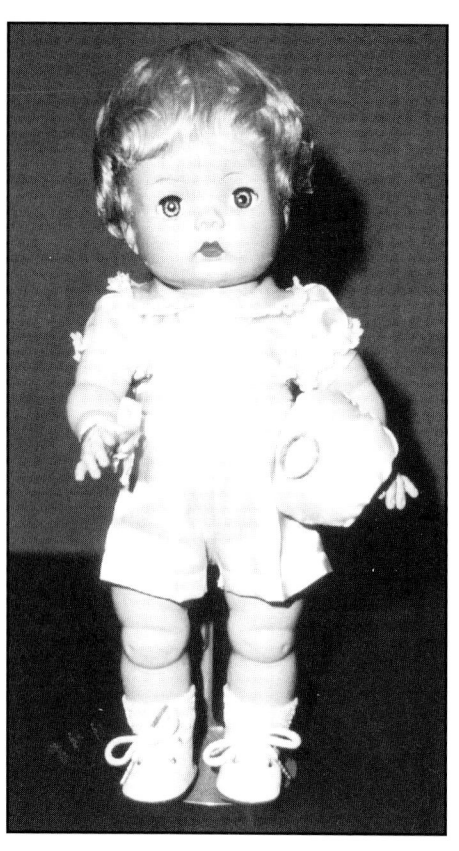

Dolls can be good investments. I can cite many examples to support this statement. When my daughter finished college and was ready to make her own way in life, she wanted to buy her own condominium so that she could have her own home. She decided to sell her Lenci and *Ginny* doll collections, and these netted her a substantial sum. *Ginny* dolls for which she paid $12-20 brought $150-200. Lencis for which we paid $100-300 brought $500-1000. She not only got to enjoy her collection, but she reaped a good return on her investment. She was fortunate in that she chose to collect in two doll areas which appreciated quickly in value. It was not a deliberate plan. She simply picked two different types of dolls that she really liked.

12in (31 cm) Madame Alexander hard plastic *Ring Bearer*, all original and in excellent unplayed with condition; seldom found. Ca. 1948-1950. *Jensen's Antique Dolls.*

However, don't think that every doll purchase will benefit from as much luck as this. I really never advise buying dolls strictly as an investment. I think you should collect because you like it and enjoy the hobby. Collecting dolls is just like collecting in any other field – figurines, books, glass or paintings, for example. If an item increases in value, I consider that a bonus to collecting, not the reason for collecting. We col-

> *Buy dolls because you love them –*
> *a value increase is a bonus!*

lect because we enjoy it. We are tempted, however, to rationalize our buying, especially with the larger amounts spent, with the idea that we are making a good investment. We hope that ten or twenty years down the road when we sell the collection, we will get more for the dolls than we paid. And as a general statement, I think this is true.

When considering dolls as investments, it is important to give the dolls time to appreciate. If you have paid a retail or "book" price for a doll, don't expect to sell it a year or two later at a profit. In fact, when you sell, you may have to accept a wholesale price; so allow plenty of time between buying and selling. In the meantime, enjoy your purchase. Remember that any field of collecting is like investing in the stock market. There are no guarantees, and there can be many ups and downs along the way, as anyone who had money in the market in 1994 knows!

9-1/2in (24 cm) *Elizabeth II* and *Prince Philip* cloth dolls by Liberty of London dressed in robes for her coronation in 1952. Liberty also made a series of dolls for the coronation of Elizabeth's father King George VI in 1939, which are also very sought after by collectors. *H & J Foulke, Inc.*

What Are the "Hot" and "Cold" Dolls in the Current Antique Market?

21in (53cm) French bisque child by A. Thuillier. This is a rare and desirable doll with outstanding wig and clothing, a choice example. Ca. 1878. *Private Collection.*

Unfortunately, there is no guarantee that any particular doll will appreciate consistently year after year. People who bought expensive French dolls during the 1980s when that market was booming are feeling the crunch because a Bru for which they paid $25,000 is now worth $15,000, or an A.T. for which they paid $60,000 is now worth $40,000. I have been in the doll market for nearly 25 years, and for most of this time it was a general rule that all dolls were making a gradual increase – some a dramatic one. But this has changed in the past five years, and the market is now experiencing price fluctuations.

Some French dolls had gone down but now seem to be coming back slowly. Early Portrait Jumeaux and E.J.s seem to have held their own and are increasing. Cloth dolls, Schoenhuts and Greiners are soft now. American cloth Chase and Rollinson dolls and German Steiff characters have fallen in price. Italian Lenci dolls are still steady. Schoenhuts will probably go down a little. The great Greiners will stay up, but the ordinary ones will drop. German character children are quite strong, but K & R 115As have gone down, as have the larger sizes of the

K & R 117, K & R 101, and Kestner *Hildas.* Some of the less spectacular Kestner closed-mouth dolls have also dropped slightly. Googlies are still rising and have proven to be very good investments. In the German character baby type dolls, those with toddler bodies are most popular. For the most part, returns on common dolls will be lower than those on rarer examples because the common dolls increase in value more slowly.

15in (39cm) Madame Alexander *Snow White,* all original with pristine matte finish. The *Snow White* face always has a lighter complexion than other Alexander dolls. Ca. 1937. *H & J Foulke, Inc.*

What Do You Recommend Buying in Collectible Dolls?

6-3/4in (17cm) all-celluloid googly girl by the German firm Rheinische Gummi und Celluloid Fabrik Co. marked with the firm's famous "turtle mark." Celluloid dolls with the turtle mark are collected avidly in Germany and Australia. This girl is quite unusual because of her googly face and molded hairdo with ribbon. Ca. 1920. *H & J Foulke, Inc.*

OPPOSITE PAGE: Large early German child by J.D. Kestner; has open mouth with square cut teeth, chunky composition body, original wig, lovely old dress. Ca. 1888. *Wayne Jensen Collection.*

As for collectible dolls, *Shirley Temple* dolls are still going up, as are Alexander hard plastic dolls and *Toni* dolls. The *Patsy* family is very popular, partly due to Patsy Moyer's *Patsy & Friends Newsletter. BARBIE®* dolls are very strong, and vintage models have made a slight increase; the markets for newer limited and special editions are very hot. Bob Mackie and Christmas *BARBIE®* dolls are especially good. *Ginnys* had leveled off, but are now climbing again. Composition celebrity dolls are still rising in price. Annette Himstedt dolls are increasing, especially the dark-skinned ones. Sasha dolls have leveled off, but the introduction of new dolls in 1995 with a $299 price tag may spur the market on older issues that can be purchased mint-in-box for $225. The Effanbee Club Limited Editions dolls have lost popularity except for *Patsy* and *Skippy.*

What About Investing in Modern Dolls?

If you are thinking of selling your collection in the future, be wary of buying expensive new or reproduction dolls. To my knowledge, reproduction dolls have never increased in value and have little resale value. The market is now flooded with cute new bisque dolls, many being direct marketed in magazines and on cable television. Very few of these will ever have a secondary market value anywhere near their issue price. Dolls that will have a strong resale value are by such artists as R. John Wright, Annette Himstedt, Philip Heath, Lynne and Michael Roche, Sandreuter, Avigail Brahms, and Ann Mitrani. These dolls are expensive, and unless you have lots of disposable income, I would suggest studying the marketplace before you overbuy. I am not saying that you should or shouldn't buy any of these dolls, but if investment is your main concern, be cautious. However, I always

8in (20cm) Madame Alexander hard plastic *Baby Clown*, all original with dog accessory. A bent-knee walker, this doll is rare and desirable. Ca. 1955. *Rhoda Shoemaker Collection.*

advocate buying what you like. If it ends up having a resale value and making you a profit, then I consider that a bonus.

Modern dolls of the last 25 years are also a risky market. We still do not know how these dolls will do in future years. I think that some of the Mattel dolls, especially those with special features such as *Cheerful, Tearful*, will eventually do well. Dolls like *Bizzy Lizzy* which have lots of accessories may also do well. The key here is to get a perfect doll – all original in the original box with all booklets, leaflets, wrist tags and accessories that came with the doll. The newer the doll you are collecting, the more perfect it has to be. The *Chatty Cathy* family is already very popular. (I just bought a book on them!) I think dolls that are sleepers right now are the vinyl Effanbee

13in (33cm) Madame Alexander composition *Flora McFlimsey*, all original. Eyes have clouded as is common on dolls of this period; some doll restorers can make iris transplants. Ca. 1938. *Elizabeth Foulke Lucidonio Collection.*

series, with celebrities such as W.C. Fields and John Wayne, the Presidents series and the literary character dolls. Dolls such as these with faces that actually look like the people they represent have a good chance of becoming very collectible.

Recent Madame Alexander dolls, once so popular on the secondary market that they doubled their value as soon as they left the store shelf (if they ever got there), have dropped to the point that dolls of the 1970s to 1980s are bringing only 25-50% of their cost to collectors. This is particularly true of the 8 inch (20 centimeter) dolls and vinyl (soft plastic) faced dolls. Dolls that have really dropped in popularity are the First Ladies Series. Once bringing $1600-1700 a set for the first six, they are now bringing $50-90 each. The complete Alexander line was looking old hat to collectors until about five or six years ago when Alexander hired new designers who brought exciting new ideas to the line. Alexander again is making some fantastic dolls. The 8 inch dolls seem to be the most popular. Collectors like to assemble series of dolls. Those that should eventually do well are the 8 inch *Anne of Green Gables*, *Peter Pan* and *Wizard of Oz* groups. The *Emerald City Dorothy*, *Wizard* and *Witch* were made in limited quantities and will be very hard to find. The *Scarlett Series* has been extensive, with many costume changes, and it continues to be very popular. We are very disappointed that the *Wendy Loves...* series has been discontinued. I think these have a great potential for appreciation because collectors love the little girl *Wendys*. Just look at the prices for those from the 1950s and 1960s. There is no shortage of new Alexander dolls, and it is possible for the prudent collector to find sales at stores and shows featuring 15-20% off regular prices.

Buy dolls that are mint.

What About BARBIE® Dolls?

BARBIE® American Girl with cinnamon hair, wearing Pan Am Stewardess uniform, very rare, Ca. 1965. Sidney Jeffrey Collection.

You can't really knock a doll that has been popular for 35 years and is stronger than ever. The *BARBIE®* phenomenon just continues to grow. Mattel caught on to the collector market some years ago. The special editions offered by Mattel – such as those designed by Bob Mackie and the proposed new Dior series and exclusive dolls offered by everyone from Hallmark to Bloomingdales – are eagerly sought after. Nobody can accurately predict the future for these types of things. Every time I get carried away trying to predict the future, I think of the Hummel market because I also collect them. In 1971, the first collector's plate was issued for $25. It quickly soared to $1200; today it is worth about $650. The collector market is fickle, and there is no guarantee of stability of pricing twenty – or even two – years from now. Currently, however, both the Hallmark and Bloomingdale editions are selling for twice their issue price. The *1994 Golden Jubilee* was selling for $1200 after an issue price of $299; it is now down to about $900. The brunette 1994 *35th Anniversary* and the *35th Anniversary Gift Set* have both nearly doubled their issue price. The *1994 Holiday BARBIE®* was in short supply, so it tripled in price really fast. Again I say, if you like it, collect it. Don't buy something just because all your friends have it or you read in a magazine that everyone should get one.

Fashion Queen BARBIE®, complete in original box. 1963. Sidney Jeffrey Collection.

If I Am Buying an Antique Doll, How Important Is the Condition?

The condition of a doll is very important in determining its price and whether or not you want to add the doll to your collection. In most cases, the head is the most important part of a doll because it defines the doll itself. The head is the part of the doll that best shows the skill of the manufacturer, designer and artist. It is the face that first draws you to a doll, speaks to you and draws some emotional response from you. If you are buying a doll with a bisque or china head, you must examine the head carefully because a large percentage of the total value of the doll lies in the head. If you are paying "book" price, there should be no cracks, face chips or repairs. With a bisque head, a small chip on the inside rim of the head, a small chip on the neck socket, a few wig pulls, a minor face or nose rub, a few black specks, a darkened mold line or firing cracks behind the ears do not affect the value of a doll. With a china head, a few minor pits, some wear on the hair, or a nick on the edge of the breast plate does not devalue it. On an antique papier-mâché doll, you would expect some lines and crazing, and on an antique cloth doll with painted surface, minor wear and crazing are acceptable. Schoenhut wood dolls will probably have a few light crazing lines and perhaps a nose rub.

As for composition bodies, it is

A 25in (64cm) German bisque closed-mouth child from the J.D. Kestner firm, with lovely creamy complexion and desirable old wig and clothes. Ca. 1880s. *H & J Foulke, Inc.*

acceptable to have some properly done repair work. Fingers and hands might be scuffed, toes might be stubbed, there might be paint chips at the neck socket and the joints. None of these things devalue the doll, and actually a few scuffs and a little dirt are preferable to a repainted or refinished body. Kid bodies should be in generally good condition with no leaking sawdust; some mends are acceptable, as is some dirt. Never use shoe polish on an old kid body to whiten it; shoe polish ruins the body! It is also acceptable if some of the metal rivets have been replaced on the kid rivet-jointed bodies. Expect the cloth body of a china head doll to show wear and possibly even have some mends. This is preferable to a brand new body. Many china head dolls do not have original bodies but do have old bodies that were made when china doll collecting was popular in the 1940s. These bodies are now 50 years old, so they really should not be disdained. It is preferable for the bodies to have old china lower limbs when appropriate. You should deduct from "book" price for a china head doll with a brand new body and limbs – probably about 25-35%.

26in (66cm) *Bébé Jumeau* by the French firm of Emile Jumeau, incised "E 12 J." She illustrates the dramatic Jumeau eyes with characteristic heavy eyebrows and deep paperweight eyes, beautiful complexion. *H & J Foulke, Inc.*

How Important Is Condition for a Collectible or Modern Doll?

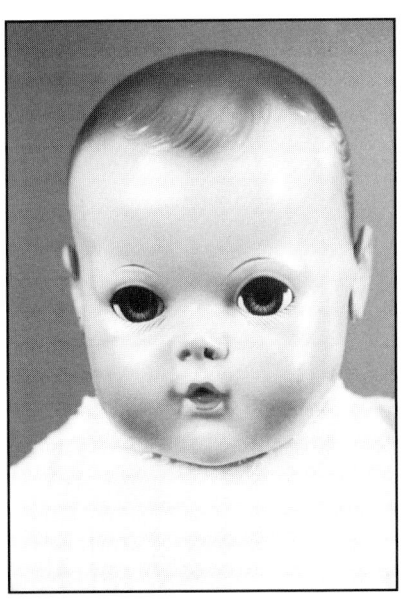

20in (51cm) Effanbee *Dy-Dee Baby*, a drink and wet doll with hard rubber head and rubber body and ears. Although *Dy-Dee* was extremely popular and millions were made, they are difficult to find in excellent condition today because they were really played with, and the rubber bodies tend to disintegrate. Ca. 1940. *H & J Foulke, Inc.*

As for composition dolls, "book" price usually requires original clothing in very good condition, but light wear, yellowing and a little dust are acceptable. Now that composition dolls are over 50 years old and more difficult to find, it is acceptable for a doll to have fine crazing, but a colorful finish is a requirement. Composition, hard plastic and vinyl dolls must have original perfect wigs in the original set to bring "book" price. The doll must be complete – wig, original clothes, underwear, shoes and socks. Cloudy eyes are a matter of personal opinion. They bother some collectors but not others. My guide is always whether or not cloudy eyes affect my appreciation of a doll. If so, I avoid them.

Condition is everything in a modern doll. It should be perfect in all aspects, including the clothing. Plastic and vinyl dolls should not have any marks or stains on the face. The collector's rule should always be: the newer the doll, the more nearly perfect the condition must be to bring "book" price and be an investment for the future.

The newer the doll, the more perfect the condition must be.

How Much Damage Is Acceptable on an Antique Doll?

This is a matter of personal opinion and acceptance. I think it would be rather shortsighted to say that one should never buy a doll with a hairline or damage. The days of having to apologize for owning a doll with a hairline are over. It is ridiculous for anyone to recoil in horror if someone says a doll has a hairline. There are lots of beautiful and rare dolls that have hairlines. The important thing to remember is that you don't want to pay full "book" price for a doll that doesn't have a perfect head. Many collectors feel, and rightly so, that a doll with damage provides them with an opportunity to own a particular doll that they might not be able to afford if it were perfect. I hate to hear people remark about what a shame it is that a doll is damaged, when it is exactly this damage that reduces a doll's price and makes it much more affordable to a greater number of collectors. For whoever buys the doll, the damage is thus luck and not a shame at all! Whenever we have an otherwise expensive doll advertised on our monthly doll list that is greatly reduced because it has a hairline, we get a large number of calls about it. So, I know from experience there is a big market for this type of doll. A porcelain doll with a crack on the face, or extensive professional repair, should be priced at only about 25-30% of "book" price. A hairline would decrease the value 25-50%; in a rare doll, it would not be as great a reduction as in a common doll. A faint inconspicuous hairline would result in only a 15-25% reduction. Personally, I would always prefer an absolutely all original doll with dynamite face and hairline to a redressed example with a mediocre face. I still think the wisest advice, especially if you are thinking of future investment, is to buy the best example of a particular doll that you can afford. However, if you like a doll whose perfect price is not within your budget but whose hairline price is, then by all means buy it and enjoy it!

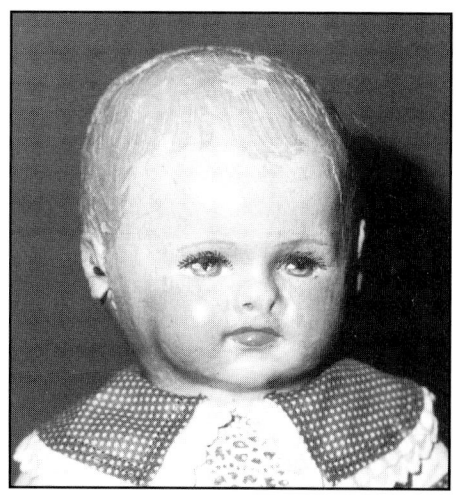

19in (48cm) American painted cloth baby by Martha Chase of Pawtucket, RI. Ca. 1900. Mrs. Chase made hospital training dolls as well as play dolls. The face on this doll is a little different from the usual Chase model. The condition is excellent with original face paint still retaining its bright color; the thick paint comprising the hair often chips as seen on his crown. *Jensen's Antique Dolls.*

31

What Would Make a Doll Worth More Than "Book" Price?

If you find an antique doll or a composition or hard plastic doll which is in exceptional all original condition, expect to pay more than "book" price for it. For an antique doll, this would mean a totally original doll in perfect unplayed with condition – perhaps even in its original box, or with a button, pin or label, or with marked shoes. It should have an original, perfect wig and factory or store original clothing. A wardrobe and/or trunk would add value. A fabulous find would be a gift set item with accessories and clothing still in its original container.

For a composition, value would be added if the doll had a perfect rosy finish, perfect eyes and eyelashes, crisp original clothing never laundered, wrist tag, box, button, pin or label, wardrobe or trunk and accessories.

A hard plastic or vinyl doll should be perfect with crisp original clothing never laundered, but pluses would be a wrist tag, box, a rare outfit or hairstyle, booklets or leaflets that came with the doll, and additional clothing or trunk.

Lastly, something that can add value to a doll but which is very elusive and nearly impossible to define is "presence" or "visual appeal." This quality can cause a doll to sell for well over its "book" value. In antique dolls, sometimes this is nothing more than the handiwork of someone who had the ability to choose just the right wig, clothing and accessories to enhance the doll and make it look particularly outstanding. The visual appeal can also relate to the way the face is decorated, the placement of the eyes, the eye color, the way the teeth are set in, the glow of the bisque, or the stunning molded hairdo with decorations. Whatever it is that makes a doll look exceptional or look like the best of its type ever seen – that quality can add to the value of a doll.

Visual appeal enhances value!

21in (53cm) Japanese celluloid doll with molded and painted clothes marked with a butterfly and number "165." She is an unusually large size and in excellent condition. Japanese celluloid dolls were originally made for export to the U.S. and Australia. They have risen a great deal in price within the last four years as Japanese collectors have started buying them. *Jensen's Antique Dolls.*

How Can I Get the Most Out of My Collecting Dollar?

6-1/2in (17cm) all-bisque *Scootles* by Rose O'Neill. Versions of *Scootles* were also made in composition and vinyl. Ca. 1925. *H & J Foulke,*

Most of us don't have unlimited funds to spend on our doll collections, so we try to make our doll collecting dollars go as far as possible. While I always advocate buying the best you can afford of what you collect, sometimes you can buy something that's only good and make it the best. For example, I recently bought a collection of German bisque "dolly faces." When I looked them over, I remarked how wonderful it was that this collector was able to find so many of them with old wigs, clothes and shoes. Then she told me that most of those dolls had been purchased unstrung and naked. She enjoyed cleaning and stringing them. She was always on the lookout for old dilapidated wigs to restore. She would even sometimes take two or three wigs apart to make one nice one. She always looked for old doll clothes. Sometimes they would have to be altered somewhat, but she didn't make any totally new clothes. Shoes were her biggest problem. She sometimes had to use new ones until she could find old ones.

For someone who enjoys "fixing up," there can be a substantial savings. At antique shops, auctions and sometimes from doll dealers, you can buy dolls that simply need a little work and are therefore less than "book" price. Finding old clothes and shoes is challenging to some collectors. They find they extend their enjoyment of the doll acquisition when they spend some time on the doll after they get it home. These collectors usually have boxes of old clothes and wigs. It's fun for them to go through what they have to see if anything is appropriate for this doll or whether they will have to keep on the lookout at the next doll outing. Some collectors enjoy finding patterns and appropriate old fabrics and trims to make clothing for dolls themselves. I know several collectors of French Fashion dolls who always buy naked dolls because they love to do the intricate sewing necessary to dress them authentically.

There is a caution in all of this, however. Be wary of buying a doll that will need to go to a doll hospital. Be sure that you consider repair costs when thinking about the price you are paying for a doll in relationship to its "fixed up" value. If a doll needs work that you cannot do, repair costs can mount up fast. Resetting eyes is a minimum of $30, depending upon what adjustments are needed; fingers are usually $10 each; joint repair would be at least $10-15 and stringing is usually $25 and up. Wigs are at least $30, and clothes and shoes probably $75.

I had antique dolls in mind in the previous paragraphs, but collectors of composition dolls can also save. We often see available collectible dolls that are soiled but have original wigs and clothes. They simply need some cleaning. If you buy one of these, just be sure that, under the dirt, the composition is in very good condition and doesn't have bad crazing. Remember that "book" price is for perfect dolls ready to put on your shelf, so you will pay accordingly for those that need refurbishing.

If you are interested in collecting a doll such as a *Ginny*, you can often save if you find a naked doll with perfect hair and coloring. Clothing is widely available to purchase separately for these dolls. However, you need to study to make sure you get the clothing from the right period of manufacture for the various models made.

Another way to get the most from your doll collecting dollar is to find the "cool" spots and collect in those areas. You can probably get the best buys on dolls that are currently not popular. When a certain type of doll becomes a slow seller, dealers are often glad to sell a doll below "book" value just to move out some stock that may have been sitting around for a while because the dealer didn't anticipate the drop in demand. Remember

Buying "fix ups" can save you money!

that dealers have to keep turning their merchandise in order to make a profit. If you keep seeing the same doll in a dealer's booth or on their mailing list, tell them you notice that they've had it quite a while and ask if they would like to give you a "better price" on it. You might be surprised with an especially good price!

When you are buying a doll from a dealer on the secondary market, always ask whether or not the dealer has a "better price" – or ask what is their "best price" on the item. This is simply a euphemism for asking them if they can sell the doll for less. Some dealers price their dolls with the intention of selling for a 5-10% discount. Some dealers put their bottom line price on the ticket and give no discount. This is an individual dealer situation, but there is no harm in asking. Always be polite about it, however. Dealers resent customers who say, "I'll give you $200 for that doll." If you want to bargain,

12in (31cm) *Campbell Kid* doll by Horsman, all original with *Campbell Soup* label. Often these dolls came in boy/girl matching outfits. *Campbell Kids* were first made in 1910; this version is from 1948. *H & J Foulke, Inc.*

simply say, "Would you accept $200 for that doll?" But don't insult a dealer by making a ridiculously low offer. If a dealer has a doll with a book price of $600 in very nice condition, don't offer $200 for it. Sugar gets you a lot further than vinegar, even when buying dolls!

Can I Buy Dolls Cheaper at Auction Than from Other Places?

I love auctions. I've been to hundreds of auctions, so I can speak from experience. You might, and you might not. The bad thing about auctions is that they are "buyer beware" situations. You have to know what is correct and not correct, or you might make the wrong buy. Sometimes what at first seems to be a dream of a bargain turns into a nightmare when you get the doll home and into the bright light. For example, a dealer friend recently bought a doll for $2750 at a large well-known doll auction house. When she got the doll home, she found a hairline that she hadn't noticed at the preview, although she had examined the doll. She had no recourse. She was stuck with the doll. I recently bought a large K & R girl at another auction. As soon as it was delivered to me, I realized that it was not on a K & R body. I couldn't return the doll because, although this auction house allowed a 10-minute inspection after purchase to check out the heads of catalogued dolls, it did not guarantee whether or not the bodies were correct. So, I lost $150 when I resold that doll because, being a reputable and knowledgeable dealer, I could not in good conscience pass off a put-together doll as correct. The point of these examples is that you must examine the items very carefully

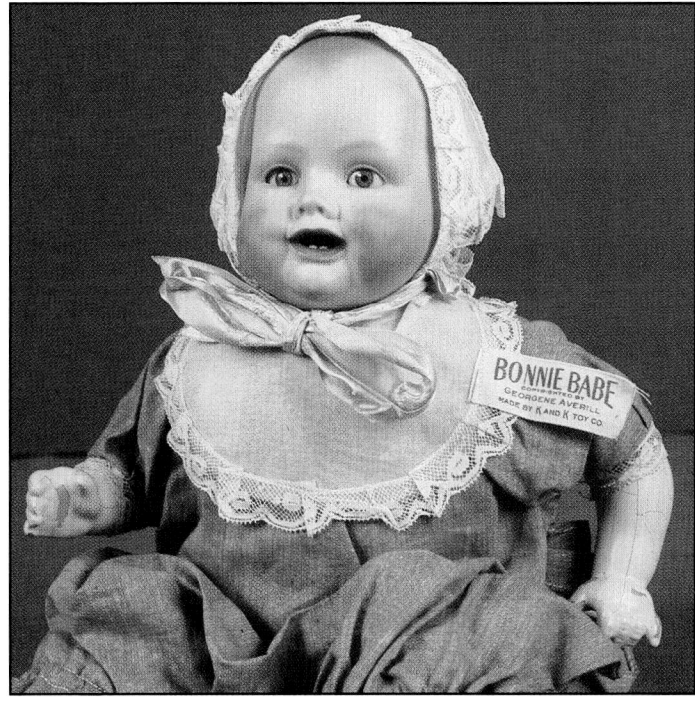

15-1/2in (39cm) bisque head Georgene Averill *Bonnie Babe*, all original with label; has cloth body with composition arms and legs, which are peeling as is unfortunately usual on these dolls. *H & J Foulke, Inc.*

15in (38cm) German bisque character boy, mold number 7760 by Gebrüder Heubach, very desirable model. Ca. 1910. *Mary Barnes Kelley Collection.*

before you bid. The lighting in auction halls is often poor, so take your own flashlight. Be wary if a doll's wig is glued tightly; it could be hiding a repair, a large chip, or a hairline.

I've also made some good buys at auction. Last year I bought two really wonderful artist dolls for a fraction of their "book" value because no one else seemed to be interested in them, or maybe they didn't know how desirable these dolls were.

I did overhear a strange comment at an auction one day. A collector remarked that she couldn't buy anything because the dealers had bought it all. This sounded strange to me. I figure that a collector can outbid a dealer anytime because, after all, the dealer is going to add a profit and resell the doll. This collector was obviously being more cautious about price than she needed to be.

Usually the opposite is true: there is a tendency to overpay. The action is fast. There is no time to think. A "yes" or "no" is only an instant's decision. Sometimes bidders at an auction are carried away in a fervor of auction fever and get into a bidding war with each other over an item. This is really foolish: to overpay for something that can be purchased elsewhere for a lot less. It's nice for the consignor and the auctioneer, but shortsighted on the part of collectors.

My most important guideline for auction buying is: **If you haven't examined the item, don't bid.** It may seem from where you are sitting that the item is going "dirt cheap." If it is a composition doll, maybe it is badly crazed or repainted, factors you can't really determine from your seat. On a china head, maybe the face is full of pits or the body is new. On a bisque doll, maybe there is a large neck chip or cheek rub, or maybe the head is on the wrong body or on a put-together. It is better to let an item go than to chance getting a below standard doll.

Auctions are fun. Don't let what I've said frighten you away. Just let my words make you cautious. The following guidelines should help you have successful experience at an auction.

1. Choose a few dolls that you particularly like and that you think you can afford. If you have $2000 to spend, don't think that you are going to buy the all-original Bru Jne or the K & R 117A. Dolls of that type would never sell for that low a price unless there was something terribly wrong with them.

2. Read the catalog descriptions carefully and examine the dolls thoroughly, including heads, eyes and body. Check the clothing, wig, underwear, shoes and socks. Even if the doll is in what appears to be all-original condition in an original box, check the clothing to be sure everything is correct and that there is a label, if the doll should have one. Dolls are sometimes redressed and placed in boxes that are not correct for them. Don't be intimidated by the auction staff. It is their job to show you the doll.

3. Before the doll comes up for auction, decide what you will pay. You may find yourself adjusting this several times as you look at the doll again and think about it. Don't forget to factor in the 5-15% buyer's premium charged by most auction houses.

4. Write the price that you are going to bid on your catalog next to the doll's number. Stick to it!

6-1/4in (16cm) German all-bisque girl, jointed at shoulders only; has molded black boots with two straps and crocheted period dress. Small all-bisque dolls are very popular with collectors because they don't take up a lot of space. Ca. 1890. *H & J Foulke, Inc.*

What Are the Advantages of Buying from a Dealer?

I think buying from a doll dealer is less stressful than buying at auction. You have more time to think about the doll and look it over. You can ask questions about the doll. Doll dealers are usually very helpful about sharing information and pointing out flaws as well as good aspects. If you discover a problem with a doll after you buy it or if a mistake has been made, you have a chance for recourse. Dealers are human beings. I believe in the essential good of people, but no one is perfect, and no one knows everything about every possible doll. A dealer may not have noticed a small eye chip or a repair on the toe. She or he may not have realized that a Storybook doll had the wrong wrist tag, or that an all-original composition doll had a large crack down the side of its torso. However, good dealers will guarantee their merchandise and take it back if it doesn't measure up to their representations. There may be a few "bad apple" doll dealers out there, but word about them soon gets around, and collectors learn to side-step these dealers.

Many antique doll dealers are members of The National Antique Doll Dealers Association (NADDA). This group screens all of their members, who must subscribe to a printed

23in (58cm) early almond-eyed portrait Jumeau, size 4, very rare and desirable, beautifully costumed. Ca. 1877+. The French firm of Jumeau created the first bisque child doll. *Private Collection.*

code of ethics. If a customer has a problem with any dealer that can't be worked out personally, the organization's Ethics Committee will help solve the problem. Many collectors feel more comfortable buying from NADDA members because of their code of ethics, but this observation is not made with the intention of downgrading any dealer who does not choose to be a member. If you would like a roster of members, write to The National Antique Doll Dealers Association, Inc. P.O. Box 50446, Kalamazoo, MI 49005-0446.

17in (43cm) unmarked French *poupée peau* lady doll with bisque head on shoulder plate and kid body, possibly with original clothing and wig. Ca. 1870. This type of doll was so popular in Paris that numerous shops opened to make and sell clothing, hats and accessories for her. *H & J Foulke, Inc.*

When you buy from a general line dealer who does not know anything about dolls, then, of course, you are on your own. General dealers usually buy dolls privately when they get other items or at house sales. If they have antique dolls, they usually sell them just the way they get them, dirty and unstrung. So, if you want to buy dolls to fix up, these dealers are sometimes a good source. I have noticed that some have a tendency to price common dolls too high because they think any doll is very valuable. Sometimes they even get more money for a common doll than a doll dealer can because some collectors believe that they will get a better buy from a dealer who

> ## *The best dealers guarantee their merchandise.*

doesn't know anything about dolls. Just last week, a general dealer two booths down from me at an antiques market had a Kestner 154 for $600, dirty, no clothes, original wig, which he sold just after he showed it to me and I turned it down. I had the same doll, clean with lovely old clothes, wig and shoes, for $495. But the person who bought his doll never looked at my dolls, although she did stop to tell me that she bought a Kestner doll down the aisle. Does this make sense?

8in (20cm) Madame Alexander hard plastic *Wendykins*, #0073 from F.A.O. Schwarz Toy Store, New York City; bent-knee walker, all original in pristine condition with wrist booklet, very desirable. Ca. 1955. *Rhoda Shoemaker Collection.*

Is Mail Order a Good Source of Dolls?

Yes, mail order is an excellent source. Many collectors live in areas where dolls are next to impossible to find. Some have bought nearly their whole collection by mail. Doll magazines are probably the best source for finding dealers and shops that sell by mail. Most dealers do both shows and mail order, but a few sell by mail only. When you are ordering by mail, always be sure that you have a return privilege. If there is a problem with a doll that the dealer forgot to mention or didn't know about, you should be able to return it. Even if there is nothing wrong with a doll, but you just don't happen to like it, you should be able to return it. However, dealers do expect to get dolls back in the same condition in which they were sent, with all accessories – hats, shoes, wrist tag, and so on. Some of the NADDA dealers do mail order, and they are required by the association to stand behind their merchandise.

I'm sure we've all heard horror stories about a few bad mail order experiences. Recently, there has been a *BARBIE®* doll scam. Some years ago there was a lady who advertised *Shirley Temple* dolls and sent out empty boxes. But, all things considered, these incidents are fairly few and far between. The names that you recognize advertising month after month are usually very reliable people. I also have heard of customers who have stolen a doll's shoes or the wrist tag, or have even substituted their less than perfect doll for a dealer's perfect one. But again, these types of incidents are few in the larger picture. Buying and selling by mail is actually a two-way trust. You trust the dealer with your money; the dealer trusts you with his or her doll.

9in (23cm) printed cloth girl with bluebirds on her outfit, still retaining vibrant color. These dolls came printed on a fabric sheet, to be cut out and sewn together. *H & J Foulke, Inc.*

20in (51cm) all-vinyl *Betsy McCall* by American Character Doll Co., all original. She is based on the paper doll from *McCall's* magazine. Ca. 1960. *H & J Foulke, Inc.*

Here are some tips to ensure success by mail order.

1. Telephone the advertiser in order to make a direct contact. Ask any questions you have about the doll. It is good to have questions noted before you call because it's easy to forget what you wanted to ask in the haste of the moment. (For antique dolls: is the head perfect, are there any face rubs or firing lines, does the doll have the correct body, what is the condition of the body, are the clothes and wig old? For composition dolls: is there crazing, are the eyes crackled, is the hair in original set, are the clothes fresh and crisp? For modern dolls: is the doll perfect?)

2. Ascertain whether the seller has a return guarantee and inquire about the length of time you have to return the doll.

3. If you agree to buy the doll, verify the price and the postage.

4. If you send a check, note the date you mailed it. If you pay by credit card, note the date. Many collectors feel more comfortable buying from a dealer who accepts credit cards because the credit card company will investigate any disputes that arise if you return a doll but do not receive a refund. In addition, credit card companies will drop dealers who are involved in too many disputes and chargebacks.

5. If you have not received your doll within a reasonable amount of time (two weeks if you sent a check, one week if you charged), call the dealer to inquire about the status of the order.

6. If you decide to return the doll, call the dealer so that the return will be expected. Return within the time limit the dealer requires. Be sure that everything that was with the doll is returned. Unless the box had been damaged, use the same packing that the doll came in. Insure the parcel. It is your responsibility if the package gets lost or damaged on the return trip. Keep your shipping receipt.

7. If you haven't received a refund within ten to fourteen days, call the dealer to see if the package arrived.

Buying & selling by mail is a two-way trust.

16-1/2in (42cm) German china head doll with 1860s hairdo, nice complexion and facial decoration. China heads with this hairdo are easily found. Ca. 1860. *H & J Foulke, Inc.*

What Should I Look for When I Buy an Antique Doll?

Ultimately, the responsibility for making a purchase rests with the buyer. It is up to you to study and to be informed in the area in which you collect. Whether you are buying from a private person, at the flea market, at auction, or from a dealer by mail or at a show, it is your responsibility to look the item over. Ask the dealer if the doll has any problems. Most dealers note any defects on the price tag. NADDA dealers are required to do so by their code of ethics.

1. First, check the head carefully. Verify the mark. Examine the quality of the bisque. Check for any hairlines, chips (especially around the eyes and on the neck socket), or repairs. Be cautious of a doll with a dirty head that may be hiding faint hairlines and cheek rubs. Make sure the head fits properly in the neck socket. Sometimes you will see a neck socket that is somewhat warped or a wooden neck plug that doesn't hug the neck snugly. These are not problems. But, if there is a large gap all around the neck, and the doll is out of proportion, that's a problem.

2. Next check over the body. It should be correct for the head. All the body parts should be correct for that type of body. You don't want to pay "book" price for a put-together doll. If the head and body do not go together, then you are not getting a doll, you are getting doll parts. The body should be in good condition; some normal wear and dirt is to be

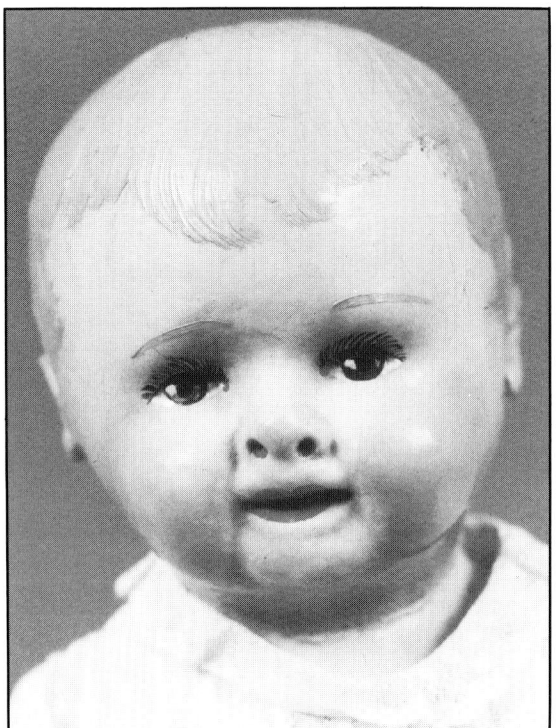

20in (51cm) all-cloth *Hospital Baby* by Martha Chase of Pawtucket, RI. Fully washable treated cloth body with nostril and ear openings. Mrs. Chase also made play and exhibition dolls. Ca. 1920. *H & J Foulke, Inc.*

15in (38cm) unmarked American composition doll, all original in patriotic costume, excellent condition and coloring. Ca. 1918. World Wars I and II prompted many military and patriotic dolls, which make very interesting collectibles. Madame Alexander even made a *Welcome Home* doll to commemorate the recent Operation Desert Storm. *Rhoda Shoemaker Collection.*

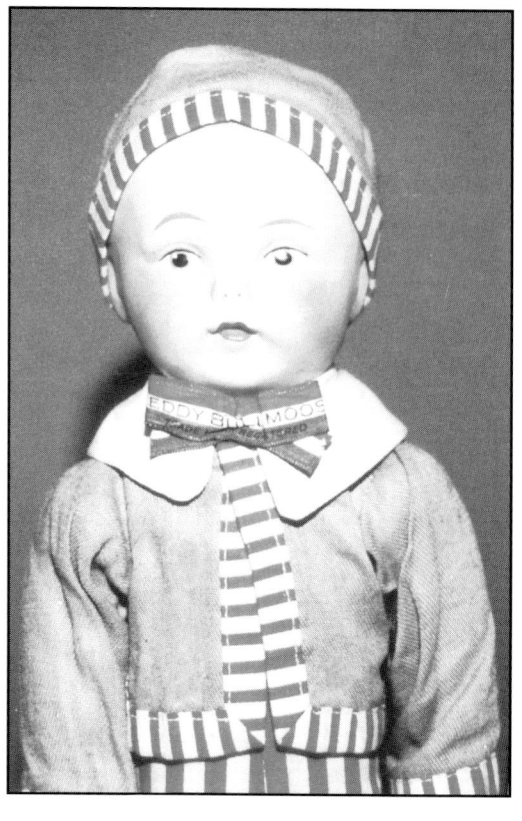

expected on fingers, toes and at joints; some repair is acceptable. Avoid a doll with a total repaint because the paint may be hiding replaced or new parts. A body in poor condition could cost more than $100 to restore if you can't do it yourself. For example, fingers are $10 each.

3. Consider whether the doll has the original wig and what parts of the clothing are old or original. It is worth a little above "book" price to get original wig and clothes. They are pluses when buying an old doll. If the doll is totally original, you can expect to pay substantially more than "book" price.

4. Consider the price in relationship to the condition of the doll, its clothing and its availability. Don't be afraid to look it up in the **Blue Book of Dolls & Values**®, which you should carry with you. The dealer probably already has! If it's a common doll in poor condition, you probably don't need it unless it is very significantly under "book" price and you want to fix the doll up yourself.

5. Remember to buy what you like, and buy the best that you can afford of what you like.

> *Be cautious of a doll with a dirty head...*

What Should I Look for When Buying a Collectible Doll?

A lot of dealers don't realize how important the condition is for a composition doll. In order to bring "book" price the doll should be clean, with original wig and clothes.

1. Check the face and body for any crazing. Avoid dolls that are cracking and peeling, unless they are very rare. Light overall crazing is almost expected nowadays, but color should be good. If a doll is colorful, unplayed with and has no crazing, expect to pay a big premium over "book" price.

If the doll is plastic, make sure the seams are secure; check the color for fading and discoloration. Don't buy the doll if it's mildewed. That can be a big problem.

2. Make sure the doll has the original wig. Madame Alexanders, *Shirley Temples* and other celebrity dolls are partially defined by their distinctive wigs. *Ginnys, Terri Lees* and *Tonis* need correct wigs. Wigs should be in very good condition. Original set is preferred.

3. The clothing should be original. Look for tagged clothing on Alexander dolls, some Effanbees, *Ginnys, Terri Lees* and *Shirleys.* Many dolls do not come with tagged clothing, so you have to use common sense in determining whether the style and fabric are old and appropriate for the doll. Also check the shoes and socks. If the clothing is not original, do not pay "book" price if the doll description specifies original clothing.

4. Check the price in relationship to the condition and clothing. I'd say as a rule of thumb that condition would be about 50-65% of value and clothing would be 35-50%, depending upon the rarity of the doll. For instance, if you have a 16 inch

14in (36cm) Madame Alexander hard plastic *Kathy,* all original with "Maggie" face; in excellent condition, hard to find. 1951. *H & J Foulke, Inc.*

21in (53cm) American Character all-cloth *Eloise*, designed by Bette Gould from the fictional little girl who lived at the Plaza Hotel in New York City; original in excellent condition with label. Ca. 1955. *H & J Foulke, Inc.*

(41 centimeter) Alexander composition *McGuffey Ana* which is totally original but the composition has overall crazing and a crack from eye to ear, then I think you can expect to pay 35% less than the "book" value of $500, or about $325. If she has flawless composition but not original clothes, I would price her at $250 – or half of book value. For a rarer doll, such as an 18 inch (46 centimeter) Ideal *Judy Garland* with very good composition and appropriate replaced dress, you could expect, for example, to pay $1100 if the "book" price of the doll is $1500 when totally original.

5. Remember to buy what you like, and buy the best example that you can afford.

With Compos condition is 50-75% of the value.

Do I Need to Keep Records of My Collection?

I think you should. But the detail that you maintain depends upon whether or not you like to bother with documentation. Some collectors enjoy making copious notes. If you do, that's wonderful. Actually, your collection notes can be done very simply. Put a small sticker with a number on each doll, or pin a small tag on the doll's underwear. Record in a separate note-

book what the doll is, when you purchased it, and how much you paid. You can go into as much detail as you want, noting what is original, any additions or restoration you made, any doll book or magazine references to the doll or maker, and so on. Some collectors even keep a photograph of each doll. This information is especially useful for insurance purposes should a doll be stolen or damaged by natural disaster. If you sell or trade a doll, make a note on your entry sheet, but keep the sheet. Someday it will be interesting to look over all the dolls that you have owned over the years.

12in (31cm) *Pansy Rose* by artist Ellery Thorpe, all original.   *H & J Foulke, Inc.*

How Do I Go About Selling Dolls That I've Found in the Attic?

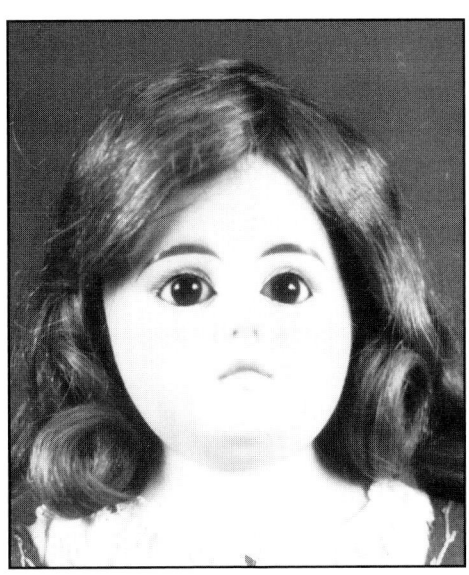

20in (51cm) German bisque shoulder head incised "L/7" with closed mouth by an unknown maker. Closed mouth "dolly face" dolls are earlier and more desirable than those with open mouths. Her body is kid with bisque lower arms; clothes and wig are old. Ca. 1880. *H & J Foulke, Inc.*

This is one of the questions I get asked the most. First, you need to identify the doll. Determine what the head is made of and the body. Look over the doll on the back of the head (even under the wig), the body, the feet, the clothing, to see if there is any name or manufacturer. If so, you can simply look the doll up in the **Blue Book of Dolls & Values**®. If it's not marked or tagged, you have a bigger problem. Look through the Blue Book to see if you can find anything similar to your doll. If you find something, read the descriptions carefully to see if they apply to your doll. If you can't find your doll in the **Blue Book**, it is a good idea to have it professionally appraised. This will involve your paying a fee to have the doll evaluated. We provide this service. Write to us for details. Some dealers, museums and auction houses also appraise dolls.

After you learn a retail price for the type of doll you have, work from that figure to decide what you might ask for your doll. You are probably not going to be able to get "book" price, but if your doll is in overall good condition, you should get 50-75% of its value. Be realistic, however, about the condition of the doll. If you have a played with Alexander *Cissy* with combed hair, faded face, dirty original clothing, missing underwear, shoes and stocking, don't expect to get anywhere near "book" price of $400, because that would be the price for a perfect doll. Your played with doll is worth only $50 because it will have to be purchased by someone who wants to restore it.

Condition is very important for old dolls. If they are dirty and unclean-

14in (36cm) bisque head child doll incised "F 2/0 G" with block letters by the French firm of François Gaultier; has early kid body with bisque hands, lovely pale bisque. Ca. 1880. *Kay & Wayne Jensen Collection.*

able, cracked or torn, they are worth only a fraction of "book" value. Bisque head dolls on composition bodies can be a little deceiving, however. The doll may be in parts, but if all of the parts are in good condition – no cracks, chips or repairs on the head – then, even in this state, the doll is worth at least half of "book" value.

Now that you have established a price, you are ready to find a buyer. Here are some suggestions:

1. **The Newspaper**. Check to see if anyone is advertising to purchase dolls; many dealers and collectors run an ad regularly. You also could run a classified ad. You will be surprised at the response you get.

2. **Doll Dealers**. Check any antique shows in your area to see if anyone specializes in dolls. You will probably get a higher price for a more unusual doll from a doll specialist than from a general line dealer, who may not be tuned into the finer nuances of the doll market. Of course, you will not get a retail price for your doll because dealers need to make a profit, but you can expect to get 50-75% of value depending upon how rare the doll is. The rarer it is, the closer you can get to retail.

3. **Auction.** you can consign your dolls to an auction. Doll magazines that can be purchased at your local newsstand have advertisements for national doll auctioneers. It has been my experience that a common doll will do very well at a general local auction; a rarer doll will bring more at a special doll auction. This is true because the people at the general auction really don't know dolls and get nervous paying more than $500 for something they know nothing about. Some people are afraid of auctions because there is no guarantee of what price you will get. Some houses do have reserves, however; they won't sell a doll if it doesn't bring the agreed upon price, but you then have to pay a buy-in fee. If you consign, always get a signed receipt with an itemized listing of your dolls so that you can be sure you are paid for each one, and that none gets lost. If anything gets damaged or broken, it is up to the auction house to reimburse you because they should have the items insured.

If you are debating whether to sell your dolls to a dealer or at auction, remember that, although auction prices may sound higher, you will have to pay at least 10-25% to the auction house; some also have additional charges for photographing and cleaning dolls. Always check on the payment policy. Some houses pay within five days of a sale, and some pay 35 working days after your last doll is sold. This latter could mean that it will be six months or more before you get any of your money.

11in (28cm) *Patsy Baby Twins* by Effanbee with composition heads and hands and cloth bodies. Totally original with bunting and clothing and even a gold cardboard tag in original box. Choice item and condition. Ca. 1935. *H & J Foulke, Inc.*

Doll Dealers buy at 50-75% of book value.

How Do I Go About Selling a Few Dolls from My Collection?

All collectors eventually find that they have some dolls that they want to sell, perhaps because they are upgrading their collections or changing directions. After you have determined what you are going to sell, examine the dolls carefully for any flaws or problems that you might have forgotten about – or maybe didn't even know about. Always point these flaws out to anyone interested in buying. Decide what you want to get for the dolls based on current market prices and on what you paid for them. Have the dolls looking as good as possible; dust or wipe them off if necessary. Locate any original boxes, tags or accessories which might be packed away in a closet.

Now that your dolls are ready, ask doll collectors you know whether they are interested in buying any of the dolls you want to sell. Another option is to ask dealers at the next doll show you attend if they would like to buy any of your dolls. Always have a price in mind so that, in the heat of the moment, you don't sell a doll for less than you really want. You know that a dealer can only pay you 50-75% of retail value, but, if you have had the dolls for quite a while, they have probably appreciated in value. I bought dolls from four different collectors during the last show I did. Dealers like to buy dolls privately.

14in (36cm) Madame Alexander *Amy* from the *Little Women Series*, early model with desirable floss hair and loop curls, all original tagged dress. Ca. 1948. *H & J Foulke, Inc.*

13in (33cm) Ideal composition *Shirley Temple* in totally original unplayed with condition, with perfect hair, colorful composition and metal button. Ca. 1935. *H & J Foulke, Inc.*

You can also consign your dolls to an auction, but check my comments in answering the preceding question because they apply to collectors also. Most auction houses won't take a consignment of only a half dozen dolls unless they are expensive ones.

If you have a lot of dolls to sell, you might consider taking a booth at a flea market or local show that allows collectors to sell. Some people have started a whole new career this way! You must check with the show manager, however, regarding any selling permits that may be required by local jurisdictions and sales tax licenses, which are required in all states except Delaware and New Hampshire. Some collectors do well selling their excess dolls at yard or garage sales. I know one collector who has a yard sale every

Continued on page 58.

Appealing dolls sell faster!

18in (46cm) all cloth *Prince* from the movie *The Thief of Baghdad* by Mollye Goldman; displays original bright color and has wrist tag. Other dolls from this series are *Sabu* and the *Princess. H & J Foulke, Inc.*

Brown all-cloth *Mammy* from the *Babyland Rag* line of E.I. Horsman. Handpainted face, all original clothing, pristine condition. Ca. 1901. *Nancy A. Smith Collection.*

15in (38cm) bisque head character boy, rare mold number 8556, by the German porcelain factory of Gebrüder Heubach. Ca. 1910. Some Gebr. Heubach dolls are currently being reproduced in Germany, so beginning collectors should be cautious when buying Heubachs, especially if they see a rare model at what seems a bargain price. *Richard Wright Antiques.*

May with regular customers who look forward to the event. I think the key to success in either of these endeavors is to keep your prices reasonable, a little under "book" price, so your customers are happy to be getting a good buy.

You can always advertise your dolls in the classified sections of doll magazines. This means that you have to ship the dolls and guarantee return privileges if a buyer does not like a doll. When your ad is published, have the dolls you advertised near the phone because collectors will be calling with questions. When someone agrees to buy a doll, get their name and telephone number. If anyone else calls about that doll, also get their name and

number so that you have a back-up purchaser in case the first person doesn't send you money or returns the doll. You must decide whether or not you will accept personal checks, bank checks or money orders and whether you will wait to ship the doll until the checks clear, about ten to fourteen days.

L'il Apple designed by artist Faith Wick as the souvenir doll for the United Federation of Doll Clubs 1979 annual convention in New York City. Bisque head lower arms and legs, cloth torso, original clothing. Collecting souvenir dolls from various conventions is a popular field. *H & J Foulke, Inc.*

17-1/2in (45cm) *Amy* from the *Little Women Series* of original dolls by Martha Thompson. Mrs. Thompson's dolls are very sought after, especially those of the royal children of England and Monaco. Ca. 1960. *H & J Foulke, Inc.*

12in (31cm) Georgene Novelties (Georgene Averill) all cloth *Irish Lass*, all original with hang tag, which is particularly desirable because the dolls themselves are unmarked. Ca. 1930. *H & J Foulke, Inc.*

Jan, How Long Have You Been in Dolls and What Is Your Insider's View of the Doll World?

I've been inside doll collecting for nearly 25 years, and we've been earning a living at it now for nearly 20 years. It's hard work and long hours, but it's fun. There are always friends and customers to talk to and to see, and new doll people to meet.There are doll shows to attend, auctions, conventions, get-togethers and promotions. There are always dolls to look at, new things to observe and learn. It's a continual process. The doll world is fascinating. There are so many aspects to it, so many directions in which to go, so much I still want to do, so many people and places I still want to see. I hope that you, too, will get inside doll collecting with me.

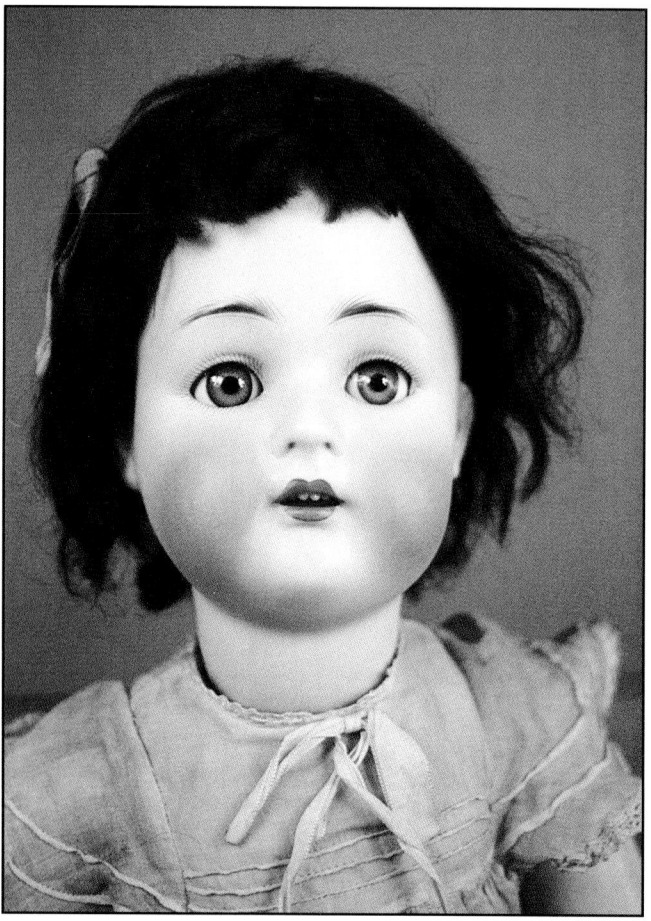

22in (56cm) German bisque child by the firm of Kämmer & Reinhardt. She has a jointed composition body with high mid-leg joint so that she can wear the short above-the-knee dresses of the 1920s without showing a ball-jointed knee; also has a short mohair wig and cotton dress of the 1920s. *H & J Foulke, Inc.*

From the J.D. Kestner firm of Germany, a fat-cheeked character baby with solid dome head and dimples. This particular face brings a premium price for Kestner character babies. *H & J Foulke, Inc.*

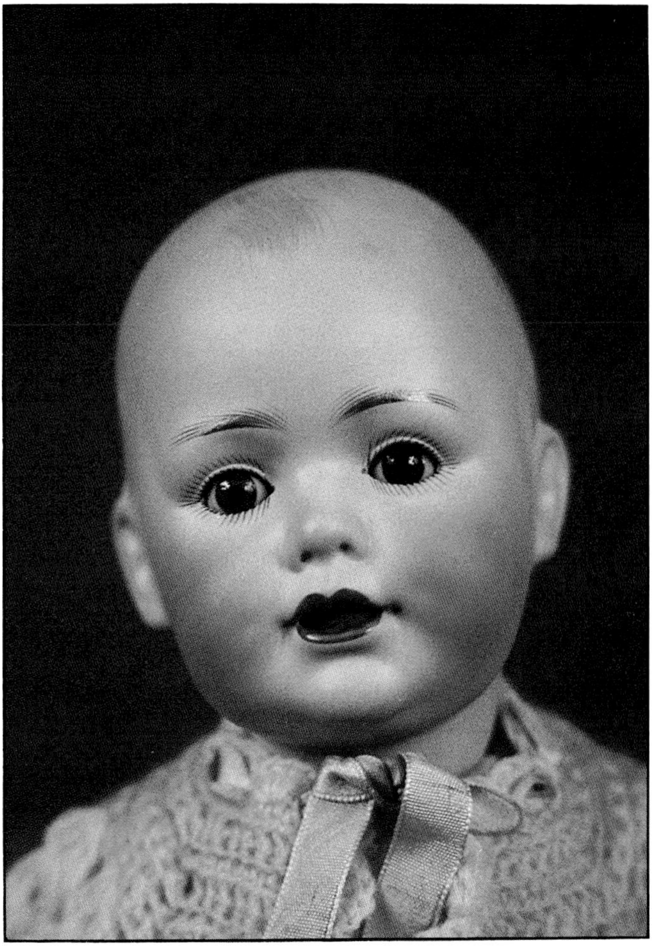

16in (41cm) early *Raggedy Ann* by Volland, in good condition for this type of doll with original hair and clothing. Ca. 1915. *Jan Foulke Collection.*

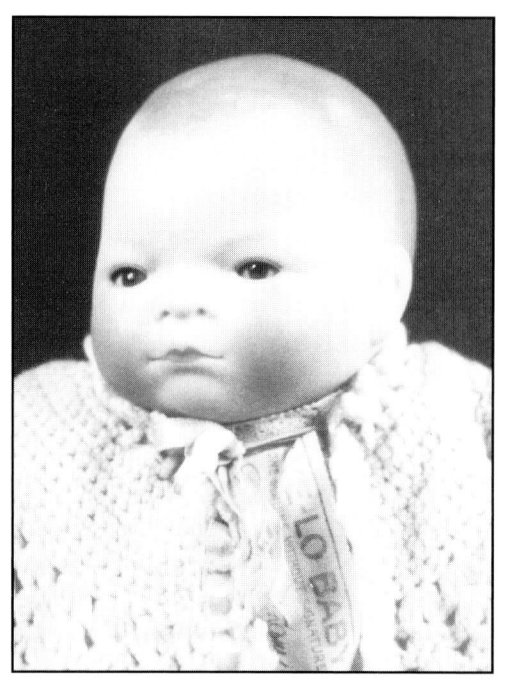

12in (31cm) *Bye-Lo Baby* designed by American Grace Storey Putnam with bisque head and celluloid hands made in Germany and cloth body made in the United States. Original clothing with label on white cotton gown. The *Bye-Lo* was also made in an all-bisque version, sized 4-8in (10-20cm). Ca. 1923+. *H & J Foulke, Inc.*

22in (56cm) Ideal hard plastic *Saucy Walker*, all original in pristine condition with wrist tag and original box, an example of a top upgrade, the best example that can possibly be found. *June & Norman Verro.*

14in (36cm) Effanbee composition *Suzanne* with magnets in her hands so that she can hold small metal objects – special doll made for New York Toy Store F.A.O. Schwarz. All original with her box of accessories, a very rare item. 1940. *H & J Foulke, Inc.*

27in (69cm) French-type all-cloth boudoir doll with very long limbs, very stylized decoration, all original. Ca. 1920s. *Private Collection.*

17-1/2in (45cm) German all-cloth dolls by Käthe Kruse, Doll I model, all original with U.S. Zone Germany tags, in pristine condition. Doll I was first produced in 1910. *H & J Foulke, Inc.*

17in (43cm) *Bébé Breveté* by the French firm of Bru Jne & Cie, lovely complexion, all original doll except wig. *H & J Foulke, Inc.*

13in (33cm) all-felt doll from the Italian Lenci firm, all original with nice color. Many other firms in Italy and elsewhere copied the Lenci dolls, but authentic Lencis are the most desirable. Ca. 1923. *H & J Foulke, Inc.*

A 300 series all-cloth doll from the Italian Lenci firm. She is 17in (43cm) tall. Her original costume shows the intricate felt work for which the Lenci factory was known. The 300 series includes dolls in everyday clothes, dress clothes, sports outfits and international costumes. Ca. 1920. *H & J Foulke, Inc.*

12in (31cm) German bisque-head boy incised "B 4" on five-piece composition toddler body, manufacturer uncertain. Excellent modeling, love those ears! Appropriate period cotton suit. Ca. 1910. *H & J Foulke, Inc.*

OPPOSITE PAGE: 16in (41cm) hard plastic *Toni Walker* by Ideal; all original in excellent condition. Ca. 1950. *H & J Foulke, Inc.*

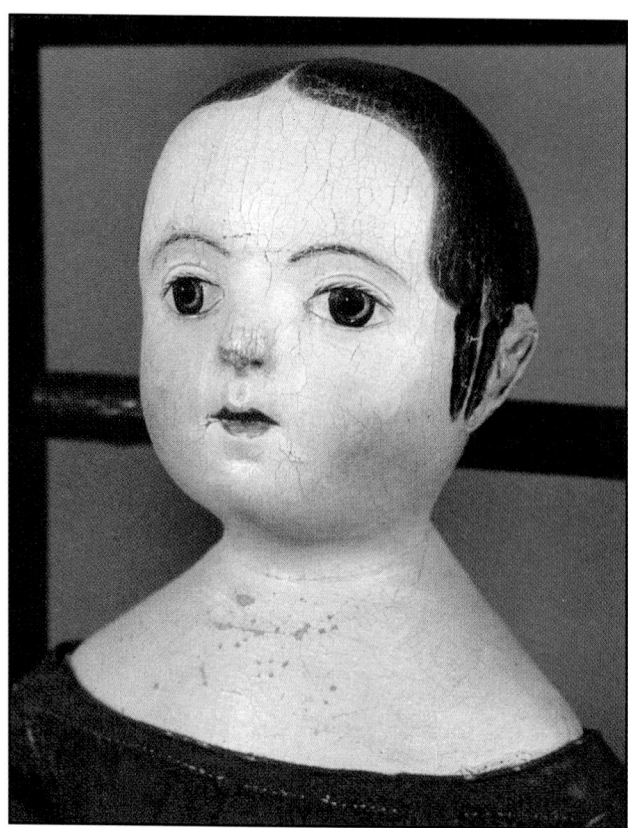

All-cloth doll by the American artist Izannah Walker of Central Falls, RI. Shows some wear and crazing as is normal on this type of doll, original bright color. Ca. 1850. *Nancy A. Smith Collection.*

13in (33cm) all-cloth Georgene Novelties *Uncle Wiggily,* all original with excellent color. Ca. 1940. *Esther Schwartz Collection.*

19in (48cm) all-wood doll by the Schoenhut firm of Philadelphia: number 314, all original and in choice condition. Ca. 1911. *Private Collection.*

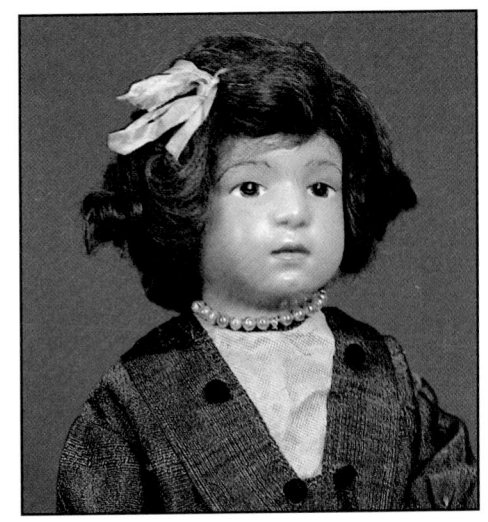

Group of carved wood dolls by artist Sherman Smith; the tallest is 6in (15cm) tall. Ca. 1960s. *H & J Foulke, Inc.*

20in (51cm) French *poupée bois*, lady on a wood jointed body – a beautifully attired example. Ca. 1870. *Private Collection.*

OPPOSITE PAGE: 17in (43cm) hard plastic doll by the Italian firm Ottolini; all original with wrist tag. She has a human hair wig and glass flirty eyes. Italian hard plastic dolls are well respected by collectors because of their high quality. *H & J Foulke, Inc.*

Ginny, an 8in (20 cm) hard plastic doll from the Vogue Doll Co. She is a desirable model with painted eyelashes. She is all original in tagged dress of the appropriate period. *Ginny* is a very popular doll because of her extensive wardrobe and accessories. Ca. 1954. *H & J Foulke, Inc.*

Jerri Lee, a 16in (41cm) hard plastic doll from the Terri Lee Doll Co., less commonly found than his sister *Terri Lee*. He has a brown caracul wig and is all original. Ca. 1950s. *H & J Foulke, Inc.*

15in (38cm) German papier-mâché lady with molded hair, kid body, wooden lower arms and legs, in lovely condition. Ca. 1830. *Richard Wright Antiques.*

16in (41cm) German all-cloth doll by Käthe Kruse, Doll I, some wear as is normal with this type of doll. Kruse dolls are eagerly sought after by German collectors. Ca. 1910+. *H & J Foulke, Inc.*

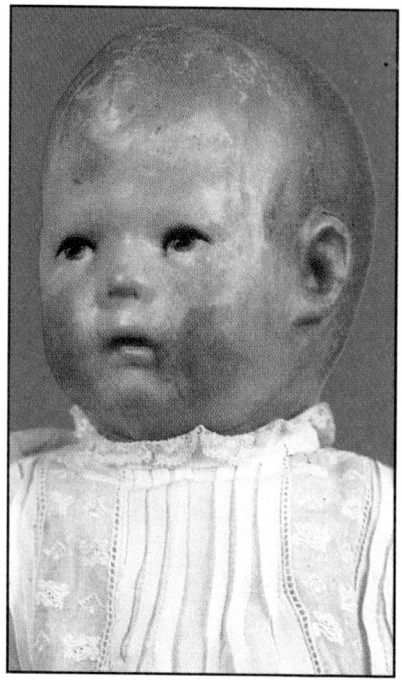

17-3/4in (45cm) doll by the English Pierotti firm with poured wax shoulder head, lower arms and legs and cloth torso and upper limbs; in all original condition with rosy complexion. Ca. 1860. *Private Collection.*

7in (18cm) doll with china head and lower limbs, a *Godey's Little Lady Doll* by Ruth Gibbs of Flemington, NJ. She is completely original. The Gibbs dolls are dressed in old-fashioned costumes of the 1850s. Ca. 1946. *H & J Foulke, Inc.*

Peter Ponsett at three different ages by doll artist Dewees Cochran from her *Grow-Up Series*. 1952-1956. Dolls are of latex. Miss Cochran also made portrait dolls to order. *Esther Schwartz Collection.*

14in (36cm) all-wood toddler from the Schoenhut Co., Philadelphia, PA. He is all original with his stand and pin. Very desirable condition. Ca. 1913. *H & J Foulke, Inc.*

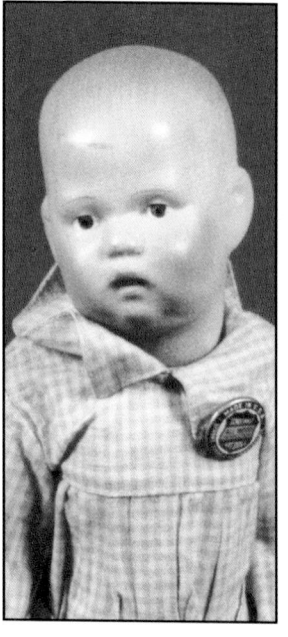

5-1/2in (14cm) painted bisque Nancy Ann Storybook Doll *Alice in Wonderland* with molded socks, all original with gold sticker. Ca. 1940. *Courtesy of Jane Mann.*

19in (48cm) English carved wood doll, with cloth upper arms and so-called fork hands, appropriate clothing, excellent condition for this type of doll. Ca. 1750. *Private Collection.*

15in (38cm) all-cloth *Ukrainian Woman* made in Russia, all original. Russian dolls in the clothing of various areas of the country are very collectible. Ca. 1930. *H & J Foulke, Inc.*

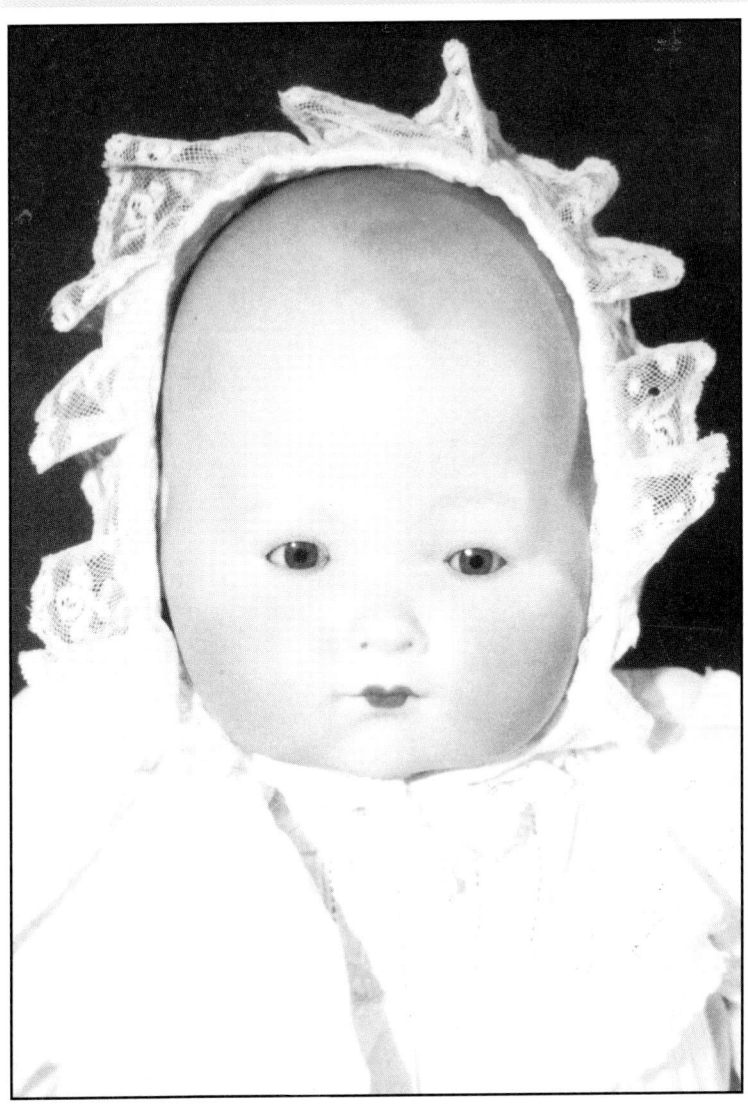

20in (51cm) long German bisque-head infant from the Armand Marseille firm of Köppelsdorf; has a cloth body. Marseille operated the most prolific doll and porcelain doll head factory in Germany, founded in 1890. This baby is from mold #345 *Kiddiejoy* specifically made for the New York importing firm of Hitz, Jacobs & Kassler. Ca. 1920s. *H & J Foulke, Inc.*

16in (41cm) Madame Alexander hard plastic *Elise*, all original with outstanding cheek color and beautiful clothes. #1830, 1959. *Virginia Heyerdahl Collection.*

34in (86cm) American papier-mâché doll by the Philadelphia firm of Ludwig Greiner. Patented in 1858 with label. The body is cloth with leather lower arms and hands, and the doll has original or appropriate old clothing. *Private Collection.*

14in (36cm) Madame Alexander hard plastic *Prince Charming*, all original with caracul wig and lovely coloring. Ca. 1950. *Rhoda Shoemaker Collection.*

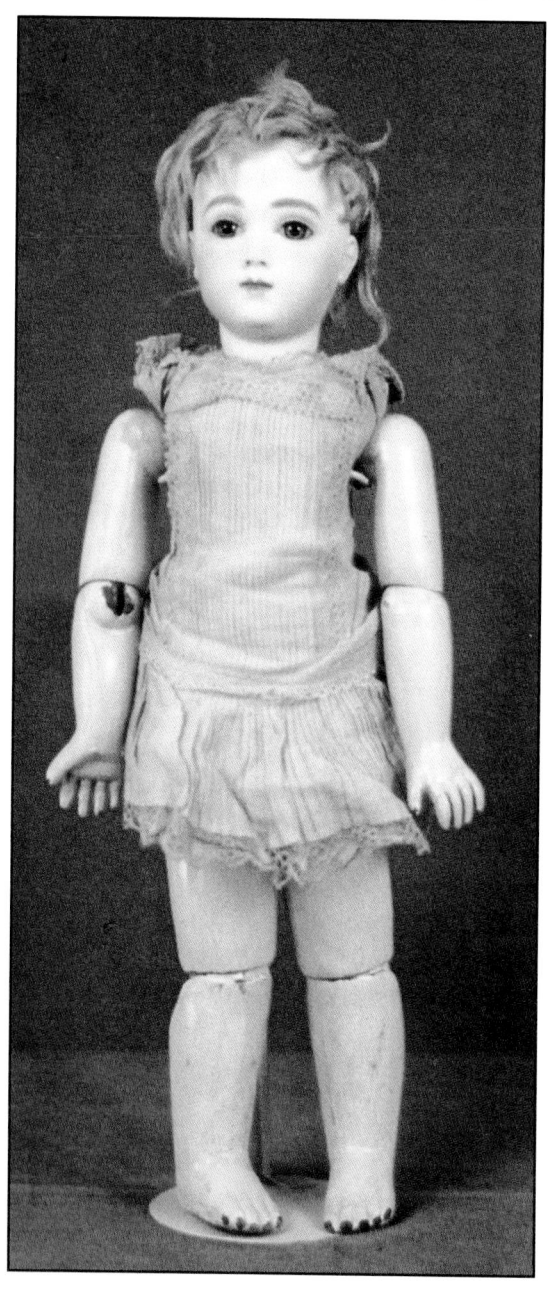

If you saw this 18in (46cm) doll marked A 9 T in an antique shop, would you pay $650 for it? If you did, you could have made a $40,000 profit. Although she seems dilapidated, she just needs some "TLC". Her head is perfect with no cracks, chips or abrasions. Her body is very good with only normal wear at joints and on toes. The elastic needs to be replaced, which will tighten her joints; this is a fairly simple process. Clean her original wig and shift, find her appropriate old clothing, shoes and socks, and she will be a beauty, the star of any collection. For proof, see her sister on page 20. *H & J Foulke, Inc.*

You could have made a $40,000 profit...!

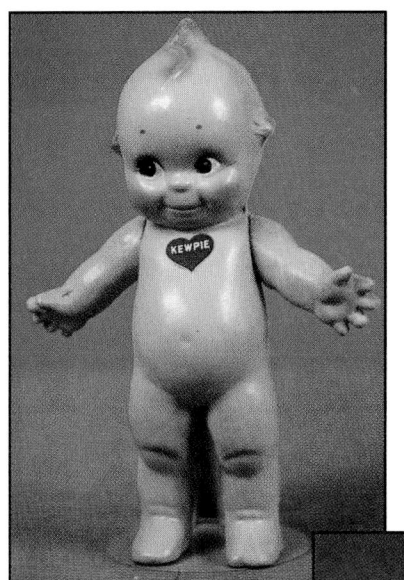

11-1/2in (29cm) Rose O'Neill composition *Kewpie* with nice rosy finish with heart label. *Kewpies*, very popular collectibles, have been made continuously since their debut in 1913 in bisque, composition, cloth, glass, metal, and so on. Ca. 1920+. *H & J Foulke, Inc.*

8in (20cm) English Old Cottage doll designed by Greta Fleischmann and her daughter Susi; all original and excellent with Design Center label. Dolls in this line represent traditional English and storybook characters. Ca. 1950+. *H & J Foulke, Inc.*

19in (48cm) German parian bisque shoulder head lady with blonde molded curls and molded hair ribbon, desirable glass eyes and pierced ears, cloth body. Ca. 1870. *H & J Foulke, Inc.*

26in (66cm) *Paula* by Annette Himstedt from her *Barefoot Children* of 1986, all original and excellent. Himstedt dolls are prized because they look like real children. Himstedt has offered new designs every year since 1986 through Mattel's Timeless Creations Division. The 1986 dolls have doubled and tripled their original value. *H & J Foulke, Inc.*

17in (43cm) Shirley Temple, 1957. *H & J Foulke, Inc.*

15in (38cm) Kley & Hahn 525 Toddler. *H & J Foulke, Inc.*

OPPOSITE PAGE: 11in (28cm) unmarked composition of good quality, nice original storybook-type outfit. These dolls can still be found in the $50-110 price range. Ca. 1940. *H & J Foulke, Inc.*

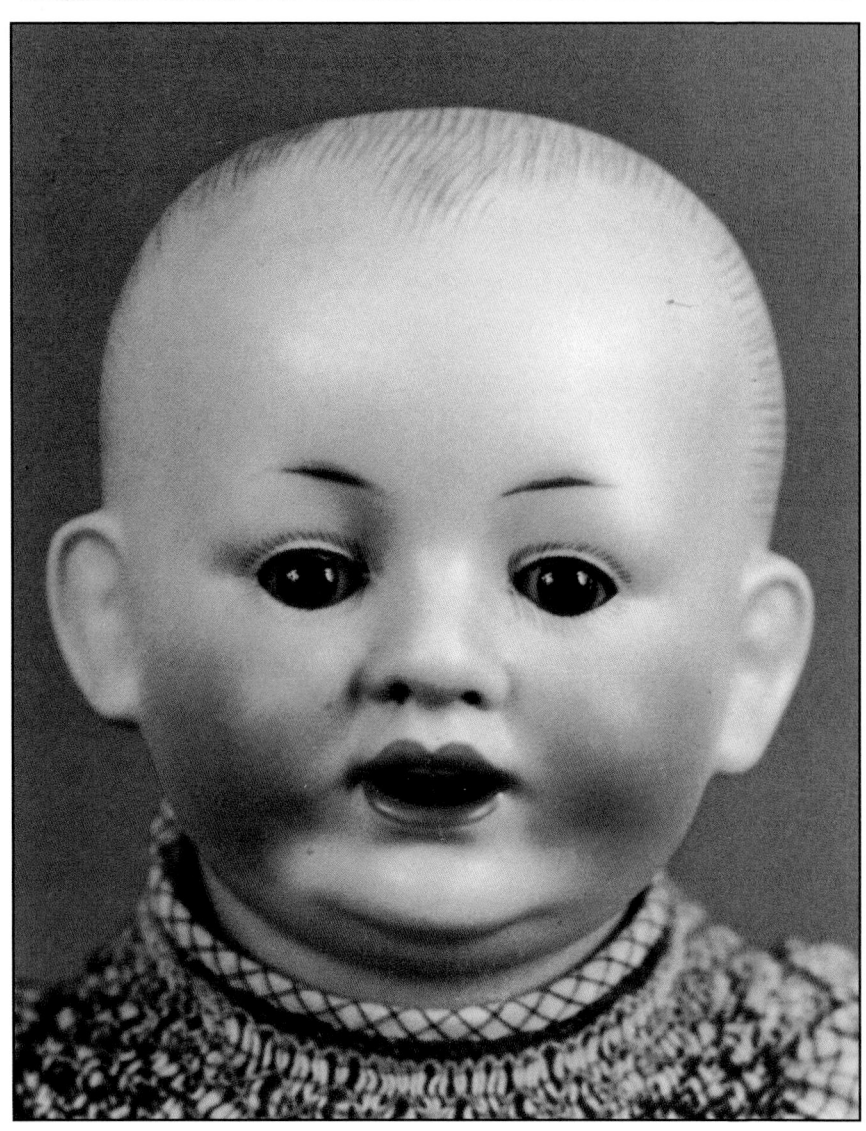

15in (38cm) German bisque-head character baby from the Franz Schmidt factory, mold #1271, excellent modeling and features, composition bent-limb baby body. Ca. 1910. *H & J Foulke, Inc.*

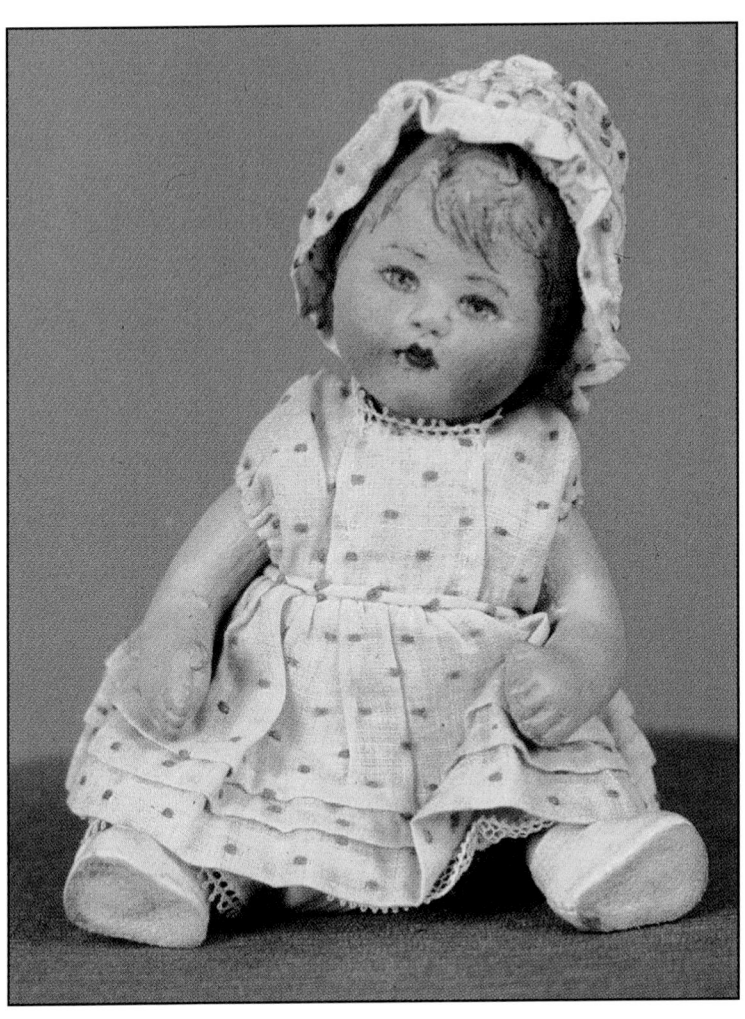

5in (13cm) French leather baby, all original with original paint in excellent condition. Ca. 1920. *Jan Foulke Collection.*

HELPFUL ADDRESSES & PHONE NUMBERS

Antique Doll World
225 Main Street, Suite 300
Northport, NY 11768-1737

BARBIE® Bazaar
5617 Sixth Avenue
Kenosha, WI 53140
(414) 658-1004

Contemporary Doll Collector
30595 Eight Mile Rd
Livonia, MI 48152-1798
1-800-428-8237

Doll Reader®
6405 Flank Drive
Harrisburg, PA 17112
1-800-435-9610

Dolls®, The Collector's Magazine
170 Fifth Ave., 12th Floor
New York, NY 10010
(212) 989-8700

H & J Foulke, Inc.
P.O. Box 1781
Lancaster, PA 17608

Hobby House Press, Inc.
1 Corporate Drive
Grantsville, MD 21536
1-800-544-1447

Mary Merritt Doll Museum
RD #2
Douglassville, PA 19518
(610) 385-3809

Master Collector
12513 Birchfalls Drive
Raleigh, NC 27614-9675
(919) 847-5263

National Association of Antique Doll
Dealers, Inc.
P.O. Box 50446
Kalamazoo, MI 49005-0446

Patsy Moyer
Patsy and Friends Newsletter
P.O. Box 939
Silver City, NM 88062
(505) 388-8989
(505) 388-5362 Fax

Yesteryears Doll Museum
P.O. Box 609
Main & River Streets
Sandwich, MA 02563
(508) 888-1711

Shelburne Museum
Burlington, VT 05482
(802) 658-3755

The Strong Museum
One Manhattan Square
Rochester, NY 14607
(716) 263-2700

United Federation of
Doll Clubs, Inc. (UFDC)
1090 North Ambassador Drive,
Suite 130
Kansas City, MO 64153
(816) 891-7040

Wenham Museum
132 Main Street
Wenham, MA 01984
(508) 468-2377

Rosalie Whyel Museum of Doll Art
1116 108th Avenue, NE
Bellevue, WA 98004
(206) 455-1116

NOTES

ABOUT The Author, JAN FOULKE

The name Jan Foulke is synonymous with accurate information. As the author of the **Blue Book of Dolls & Values**®, heralded by *U.S.A. Today* as "The bible of doll collecting...", she is the most quoted source on doll information and the most respected and recognized authority on dolls and doll prices in the world.

Born in Burlington, New Jersey, Jan Foulke has always had a fondness for dolls. She recalls, "Many happy hours of my childhood were spent with dolls as companions, since we lived on a quiet county road, and until I was ten, I was an only child." Jan and her husband, Howard, who photographs the dolls presented in Jan's many titles, were both fond of antiquing as a hobby, and in 1972 they decided to open a small antique shop of their own. The interest of their daughter, Beth, in dolls sparked their curiosity about the history of old dolls – an interest that quite naturally grew out of their love of heirlooms. The stock in their antique shop gradually changed and evolved into an antique doll shop.

Early in the development of their antique doll shop, Jan and Howard realized that there was a critical need for an accurate and reliable doll identification and price guide resource. In the early 1970s, the Foulkes teamed up with Hobby House Press to produce (along with Thelma Bateman) the first **Blue Book of Dolls & Values,** originally published in 1974. Since that time, the Foulkes have exclusively authored and illustrated the eleven successive editions, which have sold over 1/2 million copies. Today the **Blue Book** is regard by collectors and dealers as the definitive source for doll prices and values.

Jan and Howard Foulke now dedicate all of their professional time to the world of dolls: writing and illustrating books and articles, appraising collections, lecturing on antique dolls, acting as consultants to museums, auction houses and major collectors, and selling dolls both by mail order and through exhibits at major shows throughout the United States. Mrs. Foulke is a member of the United Federation of Dolls Clubs, Doll Collectors of America, and the International Doll Academy.

Most Quoted Authority on Dolls!

OTHER BOOKS BY JAN FOULKE

Blue Book of Dolls & Values®
2nd Blue Book of Dolls & Values®
3rd Blue Book of Dolls & Values®
4th Blue Book of Dolls & Values®
5th Blue Book of Dolls & Values®
6th Blue Book of Dolls & Values®
7th Blue Book of Dolls & Values®
8th Blue Book of Dolls & Values®
9th Blue Book of Dolls & Values®
10th Blue Book of Dolls & Values®
11th Blue Book of Dolls & Values®
12th Blue Book of Dolls & Values®
Focusing on Effanbee Composition Dolls
Focusing on Treasury of Mme. Alexander Dolls
Focusing on Gebrüder Heubach Dolls
Kestner: King of Dollmakers
Simon & Halbig Dolls: The Artful Aspect
Doll Classics
Focusing on Dolls
Doll Buying & Selling: The Insider's Guide
China Doll Collecting: The Insider's Guide
German 'Dolly' Collecting: The Insider's Guide

12th Blue Book Dolls & Values®
by Jan Foulke

You will find this classic identification and price guide book indispensable. The book features 516 photographs, 310 in color, of antique to collectible dolls. This is the guide that doll dealers use. With this book you are a doll appraiser! **#H4940 $17.95.**

"...the doll devotees bible"
The Washington Post

"The bible of doll collecting..."
U.S.A. Today

Save Money with any of these new books! Each book in the Insider's Guide Series to Doll Collecting is a treasure trove of tips on how to buy, sell, and collect dolls. Authored by Jan Foulke, a highly successful doll dealer, whose series of *Blue Books Dolls & Values* has sold over 1/2 million copies. Jan is the most quoted authority on dolls. Just one successful tip will get you back many times the cost of the book.

The Insider's Guide to
DOLL BUYING & SELLING:
Antique to Modern
by Jan Foulke
The beginner to the advanced collector or the antique to modern collector will find this book a must.
#H4944 $9.95

The Insider's Guide to
CHINA DOLL COLLECTING
by Jan Foulke
You will find a bonanza of buying, selling, and collecting tips for these antique dolls!
#H4943 $9.95

The Insider's Guide to
GERMAN 'DOLLY' COLLECTING
by Jan Foulke
Bisque girl doll lovers will find this book a treasure trove of buying, selling and collecting tips!
#H4945 $9.95